A Year in the Field

A Year in the Field

Apprenticeship in the Energy Arts

by

Michael Smith

instituteofenergyarts.com

Published by

Bookstand Publishing

Gilroy, CA 95020

2551_3

Copyright © 2009 by Michael Smith

All rights reserved. No part of this publication may be reproduced or transmitted in any form or by any means, electronic or mechanical, including photocopy, recording, or any information storage and retrieval system, without permission in writing from the copyright owner.

ISBN 978-1-58909-541-0

Printed in the United States of America

Cover graphic by Charles Walbridge

Back cover graphic by Patti Landres

PREFACE

Having studied personal and Earth energies for a number of years, I'd learned enough to be dangerous. Gifted with extraordinary teachers and fellowships with other explorers of subtle energies, I felt the time had come to put myself out into the field and see what it would reveal.

This book describes a year in the field, from the spring of 2005 to the spring of 2006. A year in which I barely scratched the surface of what's in my own backyard. For me it's been a wobbly apprenticeship. One that resembles waking out of a deep sleep, groaning, dazed, bumping into things. Books and workshops only take one so far. The maxim, 'You never really know what you know until you apply it' certainly holds true. I found my greatest teacher to be my encounters and experiences out in the field.

This book is not written chronologically or logically. It darts around, pulling from previous pioneers and personal revelations. No scholarly text on divination or vibrational wavelengths here – more of an experiential account of the energy work I'd undertaken sprinkled with fly-away notions, thumbnail histories, and drop-jaw discoveries.

The incidents in the book are true, however many of the actual names of people and clients have been changed or left out altogether to respect their privacy.

If there's one thing I would want readers to ︵me away with after reading this book, it's a sense

I

and understanding that there are forces in our lives, invisible forces beyond our five senses, that we interact with energetically day-in, day-out, and the quality and character of our interaction is of lasting presence because it affects our lives beyond this life.

Ever and ever a wake-up call, the energy fields continue to reveal more and more as I become less and less a stranger. Unfortunately, a lot of it ain't pretty. Like a shaman once said, "The more conscious you become, the more toxic you will see the world."

To energy explorers everywhere

IV

CONTENTS

1	Communicating the Invisible	1
2	Seeing the Invisible	7
3	Sensing the Invisible	11
4	Waves of the Field	17
5	New Demons in the Landscape	33
6	The Was That Is	43
7	Divining the Divine	61
8	Eyes of a Seer	73
9	Energy Remedies	87
10	The Nearest God	109
11	The Spirit Home	119
12	Meetings with Remarkable Energies	135

Notes	145
Acknowledgements	150

VI

1

COMMUNICATING THE INVISIBLE

A housing developer looks across a lacquered, oval conference table and says, "You're either a pioneer or a flake."

I've just submitted an energy survey report on a giant tract of land where his company plans to construct hundreds of homes. The twenty page report does not deliver happy news. Especially where it recommends they not build houses on one prime corner of the land because I found it to be a sacred site.

"But we had state archeologists examine that area and do diggings for Native American burial mounds. All they discovered were shards of old pottery."

"I didn't pick up any burial sites there either," I say, having seen the holes the archeologists had left unfilled. "No, this is deeper. This place is sacred beyond Native America."

I don't know how else to describe it to them. I want to explain how this particular spot is actually sacred to the Earth, the planet Earth, but I sense that tidbit of information will send them spinning in their swivel chairs.

Instead, I speak about the high vibratory energies sacred sites emanate, and how the best thing to do with this corner of land would be to leave it alone or turn it into a park.

In other words, I tell the people who hired me to shed millions of dollars worth of home construction. The last thing they want to hear. Not that I relish telling them. Especially seeing how in today's competitive world of colossal housing developments, stringent building codes and cardiac number crunching, it takes a bold and rare construction company to hire an energy dowser.

Although taken aback by my park proposal, these seasoned developers are at least respectful about it. They don't laugh out loud or toss me out of the meeting straightaway. They remain attentive and even begin batting ideas about. When one of the land investors reflects, "Why *do* we always build on the special places?" I want to leap over the table and bear-hug the guy.

"Exactly!" I applaud, "Why is that?"

Another developer points out all the homes built on similar looking sites throughout the region. "Aren't those sites just as special or sacred as this one?"

"Good question," I say. "And one I can't answer without checking them out." Adding that, "No one's more surprised than me about finding such a sacred site so close to home."

"Do you know of any other sacred sites around here?" an assistant asks.

"One other one." I mention a site west of Minneapolis that suburban development had begun to encroach on. I'd stumbled upon it one day while map dowsing a client's home. As I plumbed into the prevailing energies on the client's property I picked up some hefty 'guardian spirit' energy. Pulling out a larger map I expanded the survey to take in the surrounding township. A quarter of a mile from the client's home I discovered a wide intersection of Earth meridians that carried beautiful energy. Exploring the area further I realized that the intersection was located on the very site where the American Indian

Movement was founded— a place saved from further residential construction by turning the land into a small community park.

Although I don't delve into it with the developers, at one time most of what is now the state of Minnesota radiated sacred energies. Contributing to this high vibratory field is the sheer volume of life giving waters, the myriad fresh water lakes and muscular rivers like the Mississippi, Minnesota and St. Croix. The region also features a wide crystaline rift created by a chain of volcanoes once alive eons ago. Known as the mid-continental rift, it elbows out of Lake Superior, south through the Twin Cities and on into Kansas, bringing with it a higher level of gravity than other areas on the continent. And gravity, it is said, helps bring one's soul closer to the body.

Many of the native shaman and ancient peoples were keenly aware of the sacred energies in the region. Time and tribal warfare wounded this knowledge. Ultimately it fell on the deaf ears of the white armies and the broken treaties, blood and lies rained into the soil and the waters. The rapid reach and density of human habitation furnished with the poisons and waste of industrial progress took care of the rest.

In Australia, the government acknowledges the spirit of such places as Kata-Tjuta and Ulurru, held sacred by the aborigine people. They've posted big signs that state, "Sacred Site," followed by a list of tourist don'ts. If only I could plant a sign on the corner of land these eager developers are staking off to build their multi-million dollar homes. Help salvage the last vestiges of sacred energy in this area. But I don't go there. I simply repeat to them how the place needs to be respected and protected.

Dream on, I think to myself. *They're developers. Money bends every choice.*

The energy survey report I've submitted contains a number of other impactful characteristics about the land I feel important to discuss. Namely, years of farm chemicals that have contaminated the soil and depleted the nature spirits, plus a wide area of subterranean streams that emit disturbed energy. Not to mention one helluva nasty fissure about 450 feet down that anyone living above it will surely become sick, or worse. I'd gotten a rocking headache just dowsing it.

But the talk of the meeting hovers around what I profess to be a sacred site, off-limits to construction.

"Then what *can* we build there?" One of the men finally asks.

"How 'bout a sanctuary," I suggest. "A small shrine of some sort. Open air. No electricity. No plumbing."

Thud. And thanks for coming.

The meeting adjourns with handshakes and I never hear from them again.

No surprise. Why should developers, builders, architects, or anyone believe some pesky energy dowser? Invisible energies? Nature spirits? Places sacred to the Earth? What's that about? What makes one place sacred and another not?

And for that matter, why not build our dream homes *on* a sacred site if the so-called energy is so good? 'Hey, maybe we can ratchet up that price of the property on account of its good energy - the higher the vibration, the higher the value.'

And what is this 'energy' anyway?

Communicating about invisible energies to others is tricky. It's not as though you instantly see these emanations or smell them or hear them if you've been numb to them all your life. Knowing numb as well I do, I understand the difficulty getting beyond it. It's like being told about the existence of bacteria before the microscope has been invented.

With science, 'If you can't measure it, it doesn't exist.' Our scope and depth of awareness is limited to our measurement devices.

Not being a scientist sucks some legitimacy out of my aerie observations. There aren't as yet any accredited colleges that give degrees in Vibes. Nor are there foolproof diagnostic instruments to register or track these invisible energies. So, you have the perfect woo-woo situation, or as the housing developer noted, one flake's vision of physical reality.

Yet if a guy like me can become aware of Earth radiations and invisible energies surely others can. You simply need to start paying attention to your attention.

2

SEEING THE INVISIBLE

One bright, spring New Jersey morning a dozen years ago I followed wilderness survival expert and author, Tom Brown Jr. in search of animal tracks. Tom is a master tracker taught by an Apache elder when he was a boy. I'd spent the previous day with others listening to Tom point out ways to identify wolf tracks, fox tracks, bear, badger, mink, you name it. Tom gave us clues on how to classify them into family groupings by the stride of their walk, how to isolate each track in such a way that you learn all about the animal, not just their species, but their size, their age, even if they've eaten recently or if they're running on empty.

"It's all there in the track." Tom says, gruff and true.

Stopping at the trailhead, Tom glanced about, encouraged by all the nocturnal activity on the trail, "Busy night."

I stood by, staring blankly, seeing absolutely nothing but a dirt trail covered with tawny green tree litter - twigs and leaves and sprigs of grass and whatnot. Tom took a couple steps and hunkered down, gesturing with his hand toward a spot on the ground. He began to describe the animal that had crossed the trail. I wasn't listening, all my attention was tunneled downward, trying to see the track he'd found, periscoping my eyes on an elusive target at his feet.

It wasn't until his finger closed in, outlining a bitty bending of stems that I saw it -a whorl made by the heel pad. The creature's back foot had shifted the grass ever slightly. So subtle it would all be invisible if not for the angle of the sunlight striking its edges.

Once you see it, it was there all along.

Tom stepped away, leaving us to fend for ourselves. I crouched down looking around to see what else the trail might reveal. For a long time nothing. Finally, I optically framed out a two-foot by two-foot square of earth and scanned back and forth in slow figure 8's. Doing 'dirt time,' as Tom called it.

My eyes moved so slow I could see morning sunlight stretch across the land. For me, it wasn't important to classify the animal as a bounder or a galloper, or to identify it by name. I'd be happy simply to recognize a single print from the puzzle of leaves and grass. So, when a track appeared before me – a tiny bowl in the dirt - I felt I'd discovered buried treasure. I expanded out from there, and moving on a little ways another print came out of hiding. This one big enough to make out the topography of the whole track, its heel crater, the indentation of the mammal's toes, and the punctuation of a claw point.

Spellbound, I searched for more, stooped over like a farsighted man combing the earth for a lost contact lens. After an hour at this I stood up to unkink my back and, gazing down the trail, it was as if a veil had been lifted off the ground. Animal tracks rose here and there, of various sizes, depths and directions. My eyes could now see in a new dimension. Although I couldn't identify who the animals were, I could see the pockets of their steps like flowers blooming in a time-lapse film. Their spirit came to life in the prints they'd left behind. I could almost sense their feet touching the earth, some with wet paws, fresh from a nearby creek. Some on the prowl. Others, running for their life, moving their young to a new shelter. All of it written on the Earth.

This tracking experience illustrates what it's like to become conscious of Earth energies. The only difference is the animal prints are within the field of the five senses. Earth energies are more subtle, both beyond the five sense field and within it. Still, given some "dirt time," little by little the fog begins to lift on this other dimension. A dimension that was there all along.

As with tracking, you don't need expensive scientific equipment, binoculars or radar to begin to sense this other dimension. The only tools I needed to start sensing the invisible were a pendulum and a pair of angle rods.

3

SENSING THE INVISIBLE

Say 'dowsing' and one pictures a gritty farm hand striding intently through prairie grass, the two ends of a forked branch bowed taut between his callused hands.

Here in Minnesota you can toss a donut in the air and it's bound to hit someone whose uncle or grandfather was a water witcher or hired one at one time to locate an underground source of potable water on their land.

Dowsing, or divining (*), has been a viable way of finding underground water in North America since the settlers sailed the Atlantic from the old world. Today, umpteen books have been written on the subject with dowsing societies cropping up all over the continent.

How far back does it go? Thousands of years and for some of those years it's been a perilous climb against a stiff wind. Condemned by science and forced into hiding by religious institutions, dowsing has managed to pop back up again and again like some buoyant, unsinkable memory — a memory of the sixth sense we lost along the way.

(*) indicates there is more information at the end of the book in the Notes section.

Certainly in earlier Earth times, our ancient ancestors carried more consciousness of subtle energies than today. Still-standing edifices such as the Egyptian pyramids shout this loud and clear. Climbing them, one gapes in wonder at the astounding feat of erecting such magnificent and intricately fitted, star-aligned structures. Yet that's only half the story. What goes less noted is the site itself, and the awareness our ancestors carried of the spectacular Earth energies emanating from that spot on the Giza plateau long before anything was constructed.

These ancients were not only able to perceive and qualify Earth energies, and highly beneficial ones at that, they constructed living stone beacons directly on or near the spots of greatest intensity. One could say the same for Angkor Wat in Cambodia, not the temple that stands today, which is another remarkable feat of construction, but the site it is built upon.

Many of the old churches that dot Europe and Great Britain were built over pre-Christian era temples, pagan gathering places of spiritual worship and initiation. Places alive with highly enriched energies.

For many of the ancient Earth peoples, this extra sensory perception was not an extra, but an everyday state of perception that came pre-installed in their body. A sixth sense they applied as easily and automatically as our eyes dilate to see in a darkened room.

What happened? How did we lose such an inborn intuitive faculty?

Speculation would point to natural cataclysms, ash clouds, ice ages, plagues and extinctions. All plausible scenarios. Probing the distant past wearing 'human nature' glasses, it would appear we beat the sixth sense out of each other with murder, power, human sacrifice and mind control. By normalizing harm we drove ourselves into darkness and out of 'sight'.

However it transpired, we lost an enormous gift. Like losing an instinct, or a band of color from the rainbow. We lost our connection with the etheric world and barbarically claimed dominion over the physical one.

Our sixth sense diminished yet fortunately for us it did not disappear altogether. There have been those who kept the lantern burning. Gratitude is due to all these light-bearers - the ancient geomancers, Chinese Feng Shui masters, Egyptian mystics and worldly shaman who kept this lost sense alive.

Extra special thanks is due to the born intuitives who walk the narrow and skeptical planet today with this perceptual ability either all or partially intact.

Most folks are like me. We have to pay tuition for intuition. Our sixth sense has rusted shut. We need extensions, antennas, dowsing instruments to access this subtler realm. A stick or wand or dingle dangle thing to pick up energy currents and unseen radiations. Some people gravitate to muscle testing as a tool for this perception, using the strength or weakness of their fingers or arms to assess energies. Many chiropractors and herbalists have adopted this method to supplement their diagnosis. There are those who access the subtle realm with a twitch or electrical tingle in their open palms. And many who simply have "a gut feeling." It appears that any number of means are possible as long as one creates a code or sensitivity system for measuring and qualifying the sensations. The effectiveness of all these methods revolves around the clarity of the search and the openness of the sensory receptor. This sensitivity to invisible radiations is called radiesthesia. And dowsing can begin to build one's radiesthesia muscles.

What I love about dowsing is its mystifying nature. It provokes oodles of questions from the logic-minded, yet refuses to be absolutely, positively scientifically explained. It snubs its nose at all our plug-in gadgets and sophisticated technology. Which is one of the reasons it creates such consternation and disapproval. Is it the nervous system that's jerking the rod or rotating the pendulum as Albert Einstein alluded? Is it the pineal gland? Is the diviner tapping into the subconscious, the superconscious, the higher self, master guide, angels, the collective unconscious?

Interpretations confetti the world. Yet for all the theories and scrutiny, its colorful history of denouncements and mind-boggling successes, the art of dowsing remains a mystery. Let it be a lesson in letting a mystery be a mystery rather than over thinking it to smithereens. Obviously the divining spirit is not ready to tell us how it works precisely because we're not at a place to fully understand or appreciate its source.

Having read Abbe Mermet's foundational book, *Radiesthesia*, back in the '70's, for many years I carried the traditional view of dowsing as a means to locate underground water and minerals, find lost keys, or in my case to help determine the cause of the engine problem when my VW died. I didn't equate it with dimensional awareness and consciousness expansion.

Decades later, having traveled the world over, visiting sacred sites and working to feel and connect with the spirit of each place, I picked up the pendulum again and began to work with it in a new light.

Indeed, dowsing tools truly are what Tom Graves calls, "crutches for your intuition." They remind me of one of those primitive jungle bridges composed of long, sinewy vines wound and stretched over a deep chasm. Primitive yes, yet a bridge nonetheless. A bridge that reunites the physical and etheric worlds, where distance is an illusion, and where resonance and energy are everything.

4

WAVES OF THE FIELD

When most people hear the word 'energy' the first thing they think of is power – electricity to light and heat their homes. A person schooled in physics would acknowledge that everything is energy. Everything wiggles and jiggles, rippling with vibrations and waves. The trees, the rocks, the table, the pencil. Animate and inanimate forms. We live and breathe in a sea of energies of myriad motions, shapes, tempos, densities, colors, patterns, pressures, currents, sounds, emotions, and personalities.

This sea of energies is always on the move, dancing with interaction, shaping and being shaped, making up an ever-creative flux of invisible winds that play a direct and compelling force in the wings of the physical theater - in our health, our behavior, and our state of mind.

Understanding that vibrations carry information and influence is the backbone of energy work. Learning to read the information and qualify the character of subtle energy fields can start by becoming conscious of one's own energy field.

WHAT ARE YOU RUNNING?

In the early '80's, during my introductory years of consciousness work, the common question asked was, "What are you running?" - meaning, what is your personal energy field currently sending out. A valid question since the energy you're 'running' has a lot to do with the clarity of how you perceive the world and people around you. Your 'sight' may be obstructed by energies you grew up with, or by the dominant emotional fuel or belief that drives you to think and act a certain way.

So the question, 'What are you running?' serves as a checkpoint for taking stock of one's present energy state. A slew of questions follow: Are you consciously running IT, or is IT running you?' Are you giving yourself a choice in the matter? Are you running one emotion or a medley? Is your consciousness skewed by one or two over-bearing chakras? Is the energy you're putting out a mask covering something you don't wish to feel or show the world? Are you hindered by an old family energy you carry around like a rickshaw, unwilling to cast the passengers aside? Is there a hero, a mentor, or a friend whose energy field you're merged with? Are you still running a particular energy that may have helped you cope, overcome an obstacle, or speed gratification at one time, but is no longer viable?

Quite the boatload of self-diagnostic questions! Yet, an important aspect of becoming sensitive to subtle Earth energies is being aware of your own energy body. Knowing what you are currently radiating, and clearing any blockages or beliefs that may impede your freedom to see and connect with the spirit of a place.

Your energy field doesn't need to be in perfect balance or pristine fresh, simply that you're aware of it and how it may be affecting your ability to be present and mindful of the energies in your environment.

As I've come to learn, Nature lives in present time. To connect with the land, or with a tree one needs to be in the here and now. We may be the only species that can become trapped in past events, reliving experiences all over again, or racing ahead in assumptions, conjecture and fantasy about the future.

Present time is the clearest place you can be to sense the spirit of a place.

SPIRIT OF PLACE

The Feng Shui masters of old would follow the energy currents of the Earth and chart the flow of 'chi' across a landscape. They lived in a world of auspicious energy tides and Earth demons. Surveying the land in accordance with the timing and locations of the stars they would orient the placement of their ancestor's graves in an optimal way. This was extremely important since their fortunes were married to the manner in which they honored the family members who had passed on.

In many instances the Chinese would not construct a new home on the land without first consulting a qualified geomancer to inspect the site and see if the land emitted a healthy and prosperous energy for their habitat.

Still today in Bhutan, Buddhist monks and astrologers consult with the deities of the land and trace the configurations of the stars before constructing a dwelling. Property ownership is not in their vocabulary. The Bhutanese people never truly own the land where they live, they simply lease it from the deities for a time.

Many of the early Egyptians, the Mayan, Aborigine, Native Americans, and nomadic tribes were actively conscious of the spirit, or energy, of place. They sensed where not to pitch their camps, knowing if a site was not conducive to a safe or healthy stay.

They were also aware of highly beneficial Earth energies – havens, known and held secret, rich with life-nurturing vibrations, fertile fields and healing springs, and chose these places to erect their temples, center their communities, and direct their pilgrimages.

If you've ever visited a sacred site you may have experienced the enlivening energies that radiate there. Our bodies receive and respond to these energies in individual ways. Some may feel filled with a deep calm. Or a sense of self they had not previously experienced. Fears and anxieties may instantly vanish. Others may feel exhilarated, effervescent, inspired - 'in-spirit' - like breathing brand new air. 'Air for the soul.'

I recall a visit to the archeological site of Capernaum, located on the northern shore of the Sea of Galilee. Some fellow travelers and I stood in a certain spot and became so outrageously raucous with unstoppable elation the temple guard urged us to leave the ruins.

Sacred sites vary in character, geology, vegetation, life-supporting attributes and resonant energies. Some sites open up places in our bodies and minds we would not have found on our own or with a teacher, a helper or a healer. We needed to be there bodily to touch the land and receive the touch back.

All tolled, there are zillions of energies bubbling forth from the Earth, traversing wind and cloud, riding the stellar winds, hitched to cosmic rays and galactic dust spiraling in the blow-by wake of comets, imperceptible particles, beebles and nanotrons outside the human field of consciousness. So, how does one begin to recognize what is what?

One way is to do 'dirt time' in the physical world and little by little wade out to the etheric levels from there.

LAND LANGUAGE

People schooled in reading body language understand the unspoken messages another person or animal is expressing by the way they hold their body, their facial expression and the position of their limbs. Someone crossing their arms tightly over their chest is a defensive billboard for 'don't come in', or, 'I'm closing my mind to any new information', or , 'I don't trust you yet'. Once I was told to watch the arms of people as they approach me. If they're walking toward me easily swinging their arms forward and back, most likely they mean no harm. If they're coming at me with their arms stiffened tight against their sides — watch out! It's a signal that they're on the attack.

The land also has a body language with visible indicators that can signal an area of unhealthy energy. Everywhere are the footprints of energy. Not only is the topography of the land talking, but so are the trees, the vegetation and the kinds of creatures attracted to the place.

A diseased or crooked tree can be an indicator of a disturbed radiation, especially if there are a series of similarly deformed trees one after another in a line. I've come across trees whose bark is torqued and twisted around the trunk and found the trees to be growing on a strong intersection of Earth currents. Certain types of trees, like oaks, are inclined to grow more readily in agitated energy, whereas Linden trees prefer calmer earth radiations.

Areas overgrown with a single plant species or overrun by predators also can be symptomatic of disturbed Earth energies. Real aliveness is inclusive and diverse. A paucity of insects, birds, and animals are visible clues that the energy radiating there may be out of balance. The more natural sounds, the more vitality.

Studies are finding this to be true in agriculture where a single species or monoculture method of planting such as a field of corn, although more efficient to farm, will typically yield less than where a variety of vegetable species are planted.

This polyculture method, long used by Native Americans, benefits soil fertility without fertilizers and reduces the need for pesticides to kill or repel insects and disease. Whether it's a field of energy or a field of crops, its strength comes, not in numbers, but in variety of vibes. All the better to fight a blight.

It wasn't so long ago, pre-car, people lived closer to nature and closer to home. They observed the behavior of animals and insects who told them many things about the spirit of a place. Although the observers may not have had a name for specific Earth radiations, they were more aware of them in their daily lives than our more technologically advanced society today.

Studying the lives of animals and insects can tell us a lot about the energetic expression of the land beyond our five senses. Afterall, many creatures are equipped with heightened senses surpassing human capabilities - the vision of an eagle, a hound's sense of smell, the hearing of a fox. Some animals and insects are drawn to areas emitting calm vibrations, others to areas of disturbance.

After reading how some species of ants build their colonies in areas of agitated Earth energy, I checked out my backyard and found this to be true. Why would these ants create their tunneled home in such a frenetic energy? Does the agitation appeal to them or has it to do with keeping another band of ants away?

Delving into ant communities further I came across an old Bavarian custom. Prior to breaking ground for a new home, an ant heap would be placed on the land where the house had been sited to be built. If the ants left the property, the site would be deemed a healthy place to build. If the ants stayed, the people would look for another home site.

Weather predictions and seasonal forecasts have been associated with the behavior of animals and insects as well. There are cultural beliefs, old wives tales and folk sayings about the actions of animals and insects. Some might be construed as superstitious. If you see a cat do this, or a crow do that, it signifies such and such will happen.

Occasionally you come across a bit of lore that is energy-related, such as 'swallows nesting above the front door bring good luck to a home.' Replace the words 'good luck' with calm or balanced Earth radiations and you have a subtle energy observation, and a good one, especially since it involves the entrance to one's house.

In a number of instances, including one spot in my backyard, I found an energetic inclination with paper wasps. These wasps, who construct beautiful, wave-patterned, piñata-sized nests in trees, appear to have an affinity for hanging their homes over areas of agitated energy. Why is this? What is it about the vibrations that resonate with them? Could it serve as an invisible shield around their nest that repels other insects and predators?

Household pets can also show us a thing or two about the prevailing energies in and around a home.

SEE A MAN ABOUT A DOG

I receive a call from a man who claims, "Something is off in my house." After sharing some unpleasant stories of the going's on, he adds that the family dog, a large Doberman, refuses to walk through a certain hallway. "If I dangled a piece of raw meat there, he still wouldn't budge."

While surveying the man's house I discover a whirling vortex of rough and tough energy between the kitchen and the back door. I find it interesting that the vortex is not only energetic but also clearly visible by all the newspaper, mail and papers strewn around the area --like one of those photographs of a tornado where all the debris is sucked up and orbiting around the swirling gyro.

It's been documented that dogs have an affinity for calmer Earth energies and will steer away from agitated areas. This isn't true 100% of the time. Like humans, dogs can normalize the prevailing energies and make do. Still it's a good thing to note where your dog likes to sit and sleep in your home and around your property.

As dogs can be indicators of peaceful energy, cats tend to be drawn to more disturbed Earth radiation, though their health is unaffected by it.

On one occasion I'm called to check out a suburban home where the homeowner is having vivid nightmares and waking up with tremors. I'd previously surveyed the property remotely and picked up a hostile intersection of energies crossing in the master bedroom. As I enter the bedroom I notice the homeowner's cat curled up on the bed right on the pillow where the homeowner sleeps — directly on the spot of the most intense energy disturbance. As I step up to the bed to take a closer reading, the cat hisses and lashes its claws at my face. The homeowner is surprised by the cat's hostile reaction, saying she never attacks people like that. From an energy point of view the cat's action is clear. She embodied the turbulent energy of the spot and fought off my intention to change it.

This isn't to say that cats only like areas of disturbed radiations. Cats also like perches, laps, and beds, no matter what the energy. Then there's our family cat, Kick, who in the past would beckon me to the primary irritated spots in the backyard, meowing all the way. There's one spot in particular that he encourages me to follow him a lot – which is also a place where a community of ants thrive. Once Kick reaches the spot, he flops to the ground and undulates his furry body in side and back roils as if to fully savor the zone of irritation.

So what makes natural Earth radiations so agitated?

A major contributor comes from underground streams of water. Crossing streams below the surface as deep as hundreds of feet can disrupt the balance of telluric, or Earth, radiations. It does not need to be an actual stream of running water to be considered an underground water vein. There can be layers of sand particulates that water passes though, either continuously or seasonally.

Underground streams can also be the source of highly beneficial energy. We find many ancient stone circles, dolmens and menhirs erected above or near subterranean water veins.

Other contributors to disturbed Earth energies are underground fissures and faults. Cracks and cavities in the Earth's crust will transmit different wavelengths of electromagnetic radiation.

Surveying a home in the southern metro area, I pick up the energy of a deep underground fissure snaking across the property. I call Justin, a geologist friend, for his expertise.

"I'm picking up a nasty subterranean fissure energy about 500 feet down. Does this make sense?"

"Oh, yeah," he says, "There's a lot of fissures down there around the Minnesota River bluffs."

Subterranean fissures, faults and cavities can disrupt the natural earth radiations in a seriously unhealthy way. This one is a stinker. I track its course, where its rattling energy enters the property and crooks down the slope straight into the center of the neighboring house. *"Ouch,"* I cringe; hoping in my mind the people living in the neighboring house spend their time out of harm's way.

After sharing this and other findings with my clients, the Clarks, I ask them a list of questions about their experience living there, knowledge of previous occupants, the health history of the neighborhood, as far as they know. Ms. Clark shares how she has trouble sleeping and when her granddaughter visits for a sleepover, the child wakes up screaming in pain in the middle of the night.

"There was a suicide in the house," Ms. Clark informs me. "Someone in the family who lived here before we bought it." Then she adds, "Oh, and there was a suicide in the next house, too." *Gulp.* In fact there have been at least four suicides in the neighborhood. All kids in their late teens, early twenties."

Can the energy emanating from an underground fissure cause someone to take their own life? Perhaps not. But it can be a persistent irritant that can exacerbate existing imbalances in our lives.

Not all underground fissures and faults radiate disturbed energy. Surveying a backyard in the western suburbs I find an underground fissure that carries surprisingly pleasant energy.

Other contributors to telluric, or Earth-based imbalances come from cavities in the Earth's crust, certain subterranean mineral deposits, and the anti-magnetic energy that can radiate from the imploded calderas of ancient volcanoes.

These naturally distorted radiations have been given many names. The one catch-all term that seems to be universally acknowledged is 'Geopathic Stress Zones.' From the Greek, geo = earth, pathos = suffering and stress, which needs no translation. In other words, these particular Earth radiations may bring stress and suffering to one's body, one's state of mind or the health and prosperity of one's business. These are the Earth demons the Chinese geomancers detected and sought to avoid.

There are a number of descriptions used to illustrate the difference between geopathic stress zones and calmer, healthy Earth radiations. These include the analogy of tuning a radio to a clear channel or signal (beneficial energy) and the static between channels (disturbed energy). You may also hear people use terms such as coherence and incoherence, order and chaos, flow and blockage, harmony and disharmony.

It's important to note that unhealthy Earth energies or geopathic stress zones may not be unhealthy to all life forms. What I refer to as unhealthy Earth energies are those that are detrimental to the human condition. These unhealthy Earth energies not only rise from underground streams and faults, they can also merge with the Earth energy meridians of the global grid and spread from the site or origin.

THE GLOBAL GRID

Picture the world wrapped in living plaid. Bands of energy currents crossing and crisscrossing continents. Today more and more scientists are realizing there is an energy cartography of the planet, a geomantic quilt that can be mapped in big broad strokes down to a fine web of intersecting streams.

Just as acupuncture shows how our bodies are threaded with meridians and energy exchange points – so too, the planet Earth is woven with energy currents and nodes. Acupuncturists work to balance painful areas in the body that may be the result of blocked meridians or areas of diminished energy flow. When a nerve is pinched, the end organ loses nourishment. The same thing happens with the meridians of the Earth.

Like planet, like body.

In the 1930's and 1940's German scientists and physicians began detecting and charting the primary currents of telluric energy on a worldwide scale. Dr. Ernst Hartmann, MD, discovered a grid of energy lines running North to South and East to West in a fairly uniform, rectangular pattern.

One day I mapped the Hartmann Grid in my front lawn with bright yellow construction tape. If you want to meet neighbors you never knew you had, try something like this in your front yard.

The width and intensity of these energy lines accordion with the waxing and waning of the moon. I measured a Hartmann meridian line in my backyard that swelled from about 7 inches wide at the new moon to nearly two feet at full moon.

There's been a heap of speculation over the years among psychologists and behavioral sociologists about the influence of the full moon with intensified shifts in human conduct, a rise in domestic abuse, homicides, suicides, mental illness, fertility, along with so-called luna-tics and werewolves of legend. Since we're standing, sitting and sleeping on these energy currents, their lunar inflation may affect our emotions and urges as much as the moon's tug on the tides and the waters in our bodies. (An interesting scientific study, if one is so moved.)

The Hartmann meridians are not perfectly equidistant from each other as they network the land. They can vary from region to region, and tend to parallel the contours and topography of the landscape as they round the planet and converge at the poles.

Two other Germans, Dr. Wittman and his colleague Dr. Manfred Curry discovered another global grid. Called the Curry Net or Curry Grid, this energy pattern runs diagonal to the Hartmann Grid— Northeast to Southwest and Southeast to Northwest. The Curry Net is slightly wider than the Hartmann and if my local exploration is any indication, more uniformly square.

There are countless other energy rays, patterns, sky beams, overgrounds, leys, spirals and sinks emanating from the planet Earth. In the spirit of simplicity, I'm going to concentrate on the Hartmann and Curry meridian network. Together, they form a matrix that serves as a valuable entry point when surveying a property or a structure.

As you become more familiar and sensitive to these currents, you may feel a bodily sensation while passing through their field. For me it's a subtle pressure, as though the air molecules become slightly more compressed, or expressive in my sinuses and inner ears.

Once you sense them, they were there all along.

What continues to impress me about these energy meridians is how alive they are. How they interact with and absorb their immediate surroundings on multiple levels – elementally, chemically, mentally, emotionally, electromagnetically and traumatically. They convey and radiate the energies they absorb much like a river transports leaves and debris that drop or blow into it as it flows across the land.

In keeping with the river analogy, these meridians can carry natural life-nourishing and healthy energies through the landscape. Yet once they cross or intersect with a stronger, distorted energy field, for instance an underground fissure, they can become imbalanced and convey this imbalance along until it is neutralized or transformed. Likewise, a disturbed energy current can meet up with a more robust beneficial source of energy and be neutralized.

NO FENCES, NO WALLS

These energy meridians and other radiations penetrate almost everything. A lake of ice two feet thick, a stony mountain, and deep sea. There are no fences or walls that can block these energies from passing through our lives. No wall is high enough or wide enough. You can pour a concrete floor over them and they will pass. It's energy. You can be on the 20th floor of a high rise and they will be there.

With this planetary weaving of energy currents in mind, we can now look at the landscape with new eyes. An energyscape, so to speak. The simple, everyday routines of merely walking around actually involve interacting with a multi-dimensional energy atmosphere. We are not only passing through these streams and energy partitions, we are participating in their lives and they in ours. The energy our bodies are 'running' is continually interfacing with these invisible currents and sharing subtle or emphatic messages that can influence each other's energy state.

An essential thing to understand about geopathic stress zones and areas radiating disturbed energies is their impact on human health. The Europeans are decades ahead of America in this area.

HEALTH RISKS

Briefly, studies in the field of health have shown that prolonged exposure to geopathic stress zones can have a detrimental effect on the human metabolism, as well as one's immune system, brain and central nervous system. Numerous illnesses, such as cancer, leukemia, chronic fatigue, heart attacks, migraines and arthritis, along with nervous and emotional disorders are associated with people exposed to geopathic stress over extended periods of time. Geopathic stress is not known to directly cause these illnesses; but rather weakens one's immune system making it difficult for the body to combat them.

There have been numerous compelling findings from studies conducted on the effect of disturbed Earth radiations and human health throughout the 20th century from Baron Von Pohl to Dr. Hans Nieper. I don't need to echo them here, though I feel moved to share a grain of Kathe Bachler's investigative work.

In 1976 an Austrian school teacher named Kathe Bachler published a book entitled, *Earth Radiations*. The book details her research in and around Salzburg on the dramatic health effects of sleeping over geopathic stress zones. Ms. Bachler wanted to find out if there was a measurable correlation between Earth energies and the academic failures in children of school age. 3,000 case studies later, she not only discovered a direct connection between failures at school with sleeping over geopathic stress zones, but also ill health, sleep disorders, and death.

Ms Bachler writes, "Changing the position of the bed can sometimes bring about a swift and complete recovery. Recovery may take longer depending on one's length of exposure."

THE BED FIELD

The bed is such a vital and vulnerable place in one's life. It is the site where your body lies for hours in slumber, to repair, restore and refresh. For this duration of time your body is open to the energies radiating under it, through it and around it. This place and state of repose is also the doorway for the comings and goings of your soul. The prevailing energies of this bed field can affect the quality of your arrival and departure as well as your health.

If you know someone who suffers from insomnia, morning fatigue, recurring nightmares, depression, or sluggish development, it may be because their bed is located on an unhealthy meridian or positioned in a geopathic stress zone.

Another tell tale sign of sleeping in a troubled energy field can be when a person's malady is treated and seemingly healed, yet returns again and again. This recurrence can be because their body is being re-irritated each time it is exposed to the unhealthy energies emanating around their bed.

So, what do you do if you or someone you know suffers from such symptoms? A simple exercise would be to move their bed and see if their symptoms disappear.

Of the numerous factors affecting one's health and one's sleep, the most overlooked is the agitated energy emanating around the bed of the sleeper. The source of the agitation may not necessarily be geopathic, it could be 'peopathic.'

5

NEW DEMONS IN THE LANDSCAPE

The Earth demons the Chinese geomancers once detected thousands of years ago are still around. Natural unhealthy earth radiations still arise from many areas of the landscape. If only we were conscious enough to site our homes outside of their hazardous influence!

Over the last few centuries we've added new demons to the landscape. People-induced demons, or what I like to call, Peopathic Stress Zones. The most obvious are the residual effects of our crimes against nature and humanity —air and water pollution, toxic spillage, poisoned wells, clearcut forests, strip mining, the depletion of underground aquifers, warfare, atomic bombs, genocide, concentration camps, disturbed burial grounds - to name a few.

Another impactful man-made energy comes from the electromagnetic fields spread from the electric power grid, microwaves and radio waves - what some refer to as electrosmog or technosmog, a background agitation created by our technological innovations. These also affect the flow, vitality and harmony of the Earth's energy field. So much so, it's becoming a misnomer to speak of Earth energies as such because in more and more places the effects of present and historic human activities have so infected the natural field, the ground we walk has become an amalgam of both Earth and human-made energies - a mixed-up energy mush.

I'm surveying an office thick with what I call 'uphill battle energy.' It's a stubborn energy where no matter how hard the people work, the results are minimal, and the business spins its wheels going nowhere fast. In this particular case, there's both contaminated energy meridians and technosmog, all clotted in an airless cinderblock building.

This is typical of many industrial parks, and high rise corporate offices where energies can transfer from the path of origin throughout the building by steel beam and stud construction, rebar, plumbing, wiring, and ductwork and there's no vent for it. We've all heard of Sick Building Syndrome. What's really the cause of it?

I'm surveying a laundromat near the Minneapolis airport. Walking the floor among the swirling washers and dryers, I pick up a current of unhealthy energy running diagonally across the floor from the rear wall to the front corner. It's not an underground stream, fissure, or meridian. The electrical power is overhead, so it's not buried cable. Could it be a water pipe? No, because the direction of the current is moving opposite the flow of water into the building. I check and re-check it. I question the owner, walking the floor where I'm picking up the energy. He says, "That's where the sewer line runs."

I hadn't picked up unhealthy vibes from a sewer line before, but here in a laundromat, with all the sudsy dirt, cleaning compounds and chemicals, it makes perfect sense. Interesting that although encased in a pipe, the nauseous energy penetrates the pipe and the concrete floor above it. Once inside the space, the spinning machines create delirious torsion fields of sewer radiation.

DISTANCE IS AN ILLUSION

I'm surveying a home in the New Brighton area north of St. Paul. The homeowners are a smart, loving, health conscious family. Yet I find some seriously disturbed energy in the house. After expanding the survey, it turns out the unhealthy energy is coming from a Superfund site two miles away!

A Superfund site is an area of hazardous waste the Environmental Protection Agency has deemed a threat to human and environmental health. From my understanding, the chemicals and solvents dumped at this site, stuff like trichloroethylene, are highly toxic. The chemicals contaminated the groundwater inside and around the facility. The wells were capped, but the toxic energy is still leaking upward and outward by way of the Earth's energy currents into surrounding residential areas.

Distance is no protection. You may feel safe living far away from the yuck, while it's bounding through your front door via the Earth meridians (*).

BEING AN ENERGY BEING IN A SEA OF ENERGY BEINGS

As one begins to sense the energies radiating around them, one realizes how their own body has no fences or walls, either. I am not a closed biological system that stops at the skin completely shut off from outer energies. Certainly there have been times I wished I was! Times I wanted to be hermetically sealed and protected from the unpredictable and uncontrollable outside world. Trying to shut it out is not an option –at least in my experience. Having tried to bunker myself from the world I realized that isolation is not a friend, it may whisper comfort in my ears, but gives only contraction and madness.

The reality is our bodies are wide open energy systems, responding to the vibrations we experience with vibrations of our own. All these vibrations and energy expressions are interacting all the time. Our energy bodies are in continuous communication with these outer energies, and they with us. There's an inter-dimensional exchange going on continuously whether we're listening or not. Awake or asleep we can't hang up the energy phone!

No fences, no walls, no border patrol. A person may think the headache or nausea they're feeling is from something they ate — when it's possible they may be standing in an unhealthy energy field or on a discombobulated meridian and their body is hollering, "Move!"

The energy of the site may trigger an emotion, a memory of a past event, a heightened state of joy, or a level of confusion and doubt. So many feelings and thoughts we resonate and reflect from the places we visit! How does one unravel what is one's real state from the real estate?

If you're like me your ally may turn out to be your attentiveness to what is occurring in your body's energy field. This could manifest as a subtle pressure, a cold or hard denseness surrounding you, odd smells, nausea, headache, radical thoughts, disorientation and feeling like you're losing your grounding in the here and now. I'm shifty. I generally move around as I look around all the while asking, 'What is the site telling me?'

As with viewing the behavior of animals and insects, there are other physical indicators that can signal an area of detrimental energy. Cracks in stone, brick and stucco can be a symptom of disturbed energies. These subtle energies become that physical.

While conducting a remote survey of the major energy points of the Twin Cities, friends and I discovered a line of geopathic stress running through downtown Minneapolis and through the Government Center. Verifying our findings physically we found a series of cracks in the stone walls following a meridian across three blocks. While approaching the old stone Courthouse, east of the Government Center, I thought, "No way am I going to find cracks in that solid stone building." Yet, to my surprise, the only places the stones were cracked along the entire block-long façade were located right on the grid line.

Vacant lots, trash dumps, rubble yards, ravines, and houses falling into disrepair are also physical symptoms of deteriorating energies, whether natural or man-made. Electrical breakdowns, fuses and circuits shorting out or arcing, may likewise be caused by agitated Earth energies.

A million dollar home catches fire within weeks of completion. The fire marshal claims the cause of the fire stems from a short in a halogen light. Walking the property I discover the source of the fire is directly in the cross hairs of a severely disturbed geomantic intersection.

Another electrical fire comes gaspingly close to taking the life of the homeowner. What began at the main electrical panel in the garage launched into the attic of her town home where it quickly spread. She awakes in the middle of the night sensing something wrong, and immediately evacuates the building within minutes of the flames bursting into her bedroom. Surveying the site, a wide meridian of ragged energy is found bolting into the garage and directly through the electrical panel.

Homes are not the only victims of harsh radiations. Stores and businesses can also be affected and can go belly up for just this reason. I find it interesting when a store goes out of business and the next occupant to rent the retail space follows suit. Along comes another and repeats the fate of the previous merchants. Recurring events at a site like this are red flags for something other than coincidence or poor management at work.

ACCIDENT PRONE AREAS

I became curious about the possible correlation between geopathic stress zones and accident prone areas - roads and intersections where there is a high incidence of collisions. The only thing I'd read on the subject was a paragraph from Kathe Bachler's insightful book *Earth Radiations*.

"Black spots on roads may also be due to geopathic stress that can interfere with drivers' concentration or vision with horrific consequences."

Definitely worth exploring. Especially if it can save lives.

There are numerous factors that can contribute to a traffic accident - blind intersections, poor signage, poor lighting, distractions, drunk driving, inept driving, and weather conditions, which in Minnesota can change hourly. So, how can one determine if geopathic stress, or peopathic stress, plays a role at all in this mix?

A little research with auto insurance companies reveals a couple somewhat dated accident prone areas in the Twin Cities. One of the intersections has been re-engineered with an overpass. Surveying the other designated area in a southern suburb, I discover a highly disturbed energy emission smack dab in the middle of the intersection.

I take my curious explorations to the Minnesota Department of Transportation folks, and although skeptical, they're intrigued enough to bring me in for a presentation.

While planning my talk on accident prone areas a couple questions emerge. Could a sudden automobile fatality elicit a shockwave at the site of the accident? A shockwave that remains like an icy blur in the place, laced with grief and loss. And if so, could such a shockwave have an effect on the consciousness of passing motorists, even for a split second steal their attention long enough to cause another accident?

I'd been told of a couple who fell asleep while commuting home late one night after long hours at work. Their car collided head-on with an oncoming 18 wheeler. The two were killed instantly. Upon hearing the story I couldn't shake the picture out my mind of the shock of suddenly waking up dead. What state of confusion would you be in. Would you even recognize your own death? A shock like that surely would hover in place until it is cleared and the remnant souls guided away.

My challenge is how to articulate this to a room full of transportation specialists and traffic engineers. Here again, communicating the invisible. One has to measure their words and be mindful to describe such things as energy in a way they sound scientific and credible. 'Geopathic Stress Zones" sounds like it's been sanctified by science. Terms like 'soul remnants' is not going to fly. If I say there are ghosts haunting Highway 9, I'm going to lose them.

After wrestling with this a while I finally decide to give them a straight, gloves-off approach by showing the stages of a collision and letting them fill in the blanks. My movie buff wife recommends a car crash scene from the film *Angel Eyes*. I pull still shots from the accident footage and walk the MNDOT folks shot by shot through the scene from an energetic and emotional perspective.

"This is an accident that can't be avoided. There's no time to stop or steer around it. With the screech of tires comes the fleeting gasps and sudden panic in the brain, nerves and blood of the driver and passengers a split-second before the collision. At impact, glass shatters, the bodies whip and twist uncontrollably. There's a burst of body pain and severed breath. Sirens blare. The ambulance pulls up to the wreckage. Paramedics carry away the bodies. Tow trucks haul off the mangled metal. The asphalt is swept of glass. But the shockwave - what of the shockwave the collision created? What of the stolen heartbeat and the residual trauma of fright and pain energy imprinted in the place? We didn't know we needed a gurney or a vacuum cleaner for that. Out of sight, out of mind. But not out of reality, at least not subtle reality. The shockwave hangs in the air, welded to the spot. It may be invisible but it carries a kick to it. So the question is, "Can that kick jangle the concentration of future drivers?"

"You mean to say that a place that has good energy can become harmful after a collision?" One of the traffic specialists asks.

"I believe it can. And this is what I'd like to explore."

I didn't mention it to them, but I also wished to explore how the shockwave is absorbed into the energy field of the site. How long does it remain there? Does it simply dissipate over time? Do the natural geomantic currents convey the trauma out further like ripples from a stone dropped in a pond?

The MNDOT folks select three intersections for me to survey west of the metro area. Two of the intersections they'd ear-marked for re-engineering to accommodate the sprawling population and increasing commuter traffic. The third intersection is the site of a number of accidents.

My initial energy surveys turn up some common themes and aspects specific to each site. One treatment I recommend, unanimous to all three intersections, is to re-engineer them into roundabouts, or what are known as 'rotaries' on the east coast. Roundabouts may slow the flow, but not halt it. Once drivers have adapted to navigating them, they're safer than stoplights. The MNDOT folks listen and concur, informing me that research has shown stoplights are more dangerous. Makes you wonder how much electrical energy we'd save by having less stoplights and more roundabouts.

The intersections I survey also call for energyscaping with particular trees and stone configurations to balance the disturbed energies existing and passing through the intersection. One accident-prone intersection requires a natural barrier to diffuse the side-to-side optical distractions of signage and busy frontage roads.

At one rural intersection I find the shockwave I was searching for. Here the soul remnants from a fatal accident remain fixed in the energy field of the site and the wave impacts the land around for a third of a mile.

METAMEDICS

After presenting my intersection findings and recommendations to the MNDOT folks, a vision comes to me of a new team of accident professionals who work on the energy or metaphysical aspect of a crash site. Coining them, "metamedics," for lack of a better term, I picture these folks skilled in soul-release work, who arrive at the scene of a fatal accident after the site has been cleared of bodies, vehicles and debris. Their job is not only to clear the imprinted energy wreckage, but also to help the souls, still stunned by the sudden loss of their physical selves, to pass over consciously in caring. There's first aid and there's final aid. Where paramedics come to save mortal life, metamedics come to rescue mortified souls. This doesn't have to be limited to fatal accidents, they can follow the fire trucks, crime scenes, war zones, et al.

How many souls are still pinned to places where their physical selves lost their lives?

6

THE WAS THAT IS

In the early 1980's while visiting North Carolina on a writing assignment I strolled into a park where my body suddenly became overcome with grief for no apparent reason. It didn't take me long to realize the grief I felt had nothing to do with me or my emotional state. It came from under my feet - a heavy sorrow thick as tule fog hung over the ground from the heartbreak of the Civil War. The bloodshed and loss had remained embedded in the land itself, still palpable after more than 100 years.

Today I find this all over the place.

MURDER ENERGY
While surveying the energy of a rural property from an aerial photograph I discover a spot that emits murder energy along the northern boundary. As you can imagine, murder energy is very harsh and toxic. Not an area you want to loiter around in for longer than a blink.

Walking the property the following day to physically verify my remote findings, a middle-aged man emerges from a nearby farm house with a black dog lopping at his side. He wants to know what the hell I'm doing. After I explain my task, he tells me he's lived there all his life. "This was my grandfather's farm at one time before it was sold off," he says. "The Indians would set up their teepees just east of here."

"Maybe you can help answer something for me." I pull out a clipboard and show him my aerial survey. "I'm picking up murder energy at the north edge of the property. Any idea what that's about?"

He points to a little white square on the aerial photograph, "The man who lived in that house blew his brains out a month ago."

"A month ago. That's interesting." I tap my finger on a spot 100 yards directly east of the white house, "I'm sensing murder energy over here going back about twelve years."

He takes a couple seconds to clock back in time and nods, "Oh yeah, guy committed suicide at that place, too. Hmm, that was 'bout ten or so years ago."

Two suicides, around a decade and 100 yards apart from each other. What does this indicate? It tells me to check if there's a severe geopathic stress zone or grid line carrying the trauma all the way through and upsetting the stability of those who are exposed to it. This disturbance may not have started twelve years ago. It could have been a hundred years ago. There may have been an earlier murder or massacre at that very spot and the energy has resided there all this time attracting more of the same energy wave, whether murder of another or murder of self.

Some months later I'm working in Kansas where I find this energy traveling through two properties. In both cases there had been a murder nearby and the vibe spilled into a nearby meridian and here it is years later and that energy is screaming down the block through the folks' front yards.

OUR ACTIONS STICK

Harm once done does not mean the harm has been undone. The physical participants may have walked away, but the energy is still standing there.

One would think the natural aging of a place with the seasons and solar orbits would clear the energy emitted from past events - wash it clean with the rain or broom it away with wind and time. Not so. Trauma, loss, malevolent actions, dramatic emotions and all manner of physical and psychological abuse and pain energies can become so saturated in the time and spacial dimensions of the occurrence they remain there as a perpetuating stressor until they are cleared or transformed. These denser vibrations can emanate from isolated spots, patches, vortices, or finite corridors and merge into the geomantic currents of the Earth which then truck them across the landscape through bed, bath and beyond.

I've read about remnant energies being called 'place memory', which invokes a mental image of one walking through a gossamer tableau or holograph. From my apprenticeship experience it feels more persuasive than simply a memory if it carries a force field that attracts and incites similar energy, similar activity.

Have you ever had a bruise and then found yourself inadvertently bumping and re-bumping it? Yow! It's as though the bruise sought out another jolt - reminding you 'Hey, I hurt here!' That's my sense of this. An open wound, undoctored. One that's howling for attention.

BLOODSHED

Much has been written about subtle energy fields, vibrational medicine and geopathic stress zones, but I've yet to find any studies on the energetic impact that bloodshed has on a site and on the Earth's energy field. Human blood spilled from a murder carries the energy of our emotions. It radiates the telltale heart at a traumatic moment in time. A painwave that carries both the threat and agony of the ones killed and the harmful intent of the killers. The blood dries up, yet the vibe remains – a sudden, severed bond with the physical plane and the final gasp of an unfinished life. The more vicious the energy, the more impactful and entrenched it becomes. The life information is blocked or frozen in shock due to the body's violent demise. Instead of being enriched by the information shared from a natural death and completed body-life, the land is darkened.

There may have been a time when mystics and high priests could clear the remnant energy of bloodshed from a site. Perhaps sowing the soil with salt to absorb and neutralize the land as they uttered incantations to release the souls and the suffering once pinned to the spot.

Today we place historic monuments at the site, build town homes on top, unconscious of what befell the land a time or two ago. The people living there absorb the energy. Depending on their inner nature they can become drained or sickened from the radiations, or they can become infectious carriers of the malicious energy and spread it to their world.

WALKING ON MIRRORS

Coming across a number of places that radiate past human-induced suffering nudged me to consider Mother Earth as a repository of all human actions. A porous vessel that receives not just the wind, sound, and smite expressed though our actions, but also our emotions, our thoughts, and our intentions.

I began to re-picture this world, not as a solid and stony globe, but a multi-layered crystaline sponge cake, whose energy body absorbs all human feelings and activities, be it acts of caring and creation, or acts of cruelty and destruction.

This led to an overlook vista - taking in the long haul of human existence and the amount of bloodshed and repeated pain energy soaked into the lands of this world from battlefields, torture camps, and human sacrifice - the Gettysburgs, the Auschwitzes, the killing fields of Cambodia. What is gathered in attracts more of the same. A toxic pattern develops. Troubles recur and recur and recur. And we wonder why history repeats itself.

Are we walking on mirrors where everything we do, every action, emotion, thought and intention is reflected back in our faces? I'm beginning to believe this is so. And whether we sense it or not, we're being touched daily and nightly by distant and past occurrences - as what we choose to do in the here and now will be felt in distant lands and shape future times.

What a responsibility!

Makes one question if the cumulative vibrations of destruction and bloodshed rippling off this planet attract more destructive beings to it from the dark, riff-raff recesses of the Cosmos?

HOW A HEALTHY PLACE BECOMES HARMFUL

Surely the number of human factors that can defile the energy of a place could fill the Grand Canyon. Yet the more I travel and explore the energy of various properties and sites, it feels obvious to me that it doesn't take a bomb to turn the energy of a place unhealthy. A simple act of neglect can play a triggering role. Neglect, apathy, and petty cruelty. As everything alive carries conscious life force energy why would the treatment of the land, the water, or the air be any different than the treatment of a child?

While stopping at a high mountain pass in Bhutan, I check out the qualitative difference between the energy radiating from a large white Buddhist chorten and that of some litter scraps lying in a gully nearby. Chortens, or stupas, are one of the early Buddhist architectural structures that contain spiritually significant objects, relics and sacred texts. They are located at crossroads, mountain passes, paths of pilgrimage, and the confluence of rivers. Their purpose is to balance the converging forces, and bring mindful harmony to the site.

Rinzin, our Bhutanese guide, had become familiar with my zipping about with pendulum exploring the qualities and intensities of the energies present at various sites throughout his country. So it wasn't a leap for him to understand how the simple tossing of plastic bags and paper wrappers along the roadside could diminish the energy of a site.

To see a rich spiritual country like Bhutan, which in this day and age still carries a highly vibrant life force, adopt the careless habits of the west would be a travesty. And yet, a little neglect is all it takes. As I explained to Rinzin, it is not enough to punish the perpetrators with littering fines if the trash is not cleaned up. One sees the litter and thinks, 'Since others do it, so can I.' How swiftly it mounts!

The point being, a sacred or naturally enlivening site can begin to radiate unhealthy energy with one teeny, barely noticeable, unconscious act. That's all it takes to start the ball rolling. An eyeblink of apathy. Unless cleared or transformed, one careless act can become embedded in the energetic tissue of the site. The resulting vibratory shift can then influence the state of mind and subsequent activity of those living or stopping by the site. One thing leads to another. Before long, the site embodies the darker energies and radiates them back as well as outward across the land through the meridians of the planet producing an undertow that over time degrades the vitality of the land as it attracts matching energies.

Then one brings in an act of caring, say, cleaning up the trash or planting trees, and, unless the existing energy is severe, these connective and nurturing actions can help restore the life force.

I mentioned how there appear to be as many types and sources of energy as there are human thoughts and activities, from the plethora of physical and emotional damage to the heartfelt blessings of a person or a place. What follows are a series of encounters with energies that only begin to illustrate the gamut surrounding us.

CONTROL

I'm hired by an acupuncture clinic to survey their space. It's a relatively small clinic situated on the ground floor of a larger building located on a frontage road off the highway. After treating the energy of the space outside and inside, I become concerned with a dark energy I'm picking up in the administration area of the building. A smoldering energy of secrecy and control. Unable to access the administration office I can only share with the acupuncture practitioners that the energy emitting from that area of the building is so dominant that unless dealt with it will eventually bleed in and impact the energy balancing work that's been done and infect their space.

I find the energy of many businesses I've visited to be rigid with cold and calculated energies designed solely to produce a profitable result. Seeking to be profitable and grow a company is one thing, but the manner in which the employees and customers are treated impregnates the atmosphere and defines the spirit of the workplace. It's not about the words used in the company's mission statement, it's the energy they activate. Does it produce ethical business practices? Does it empower the workers to contribute and feed personal growth? Does the energy donate to the spirit of the place?

CORRUPTION

While map surveying a home in Lawrence, Kansas I track some disturbed energy entering the property from the NW corner and plowing right through the occupant's front door. Shuffling through my litany of possible causes I cannot pinpoint the source of the irritation.

Delving further into the energy of the place I find an expression I hadn't considered before. I write to the homeowner, "I'm not picking up toxic pollution, trauma or unhealthy electromagnetic energy to speak of. What I'm sensing is a corruption energy coming from the city planners/city hall and the construction/contractor (s) of homes and buildings in the vicinity of your home. Are you near the downtown area?"

"Yes," she responds, "I do live only a block or two from downtown. Recently they built some high end condos a block away to the NW of my place. The building was made well and keeps with the downtown landscape, but the neighbors had fought to keep it out. The large condo/office space building affects the houses on the other side of the street (less light, decreased view); however, more importantly they took down a very beautiful old tree to build it. There were protests at the tree and one person lived in it to try to stop the building."

Corruption or not, at the very least it appears the city planners refused to honor the neighborhood's wishes, nor the life of a beloved tree. The fact that corruption and self interest actually emit an energy wave strong enough to become imprinted in a landscape and affect people living downstream certainly gives one pause. We can't get away with anything! It all shows through on an energy level.

THE CAPITOL

Discovering this 'self-interest" energy led me to take a peek at our nation's capitol in Washington DC. I couldn't help myself. My personal ethic is to *only* look at places where I've been invited by the occupant or owner, and are appropriate for me and my current state of mind and ability to explore. (*) So, naturally I felt an initial hesitation to survey the energy of the US Capitol building. But my hesitancy soon vanishes when I realize that afterall, this is my country, so I push ahead and conduct a distant survey. What I discover is a cross-hatching of oppositional energies in the land radiating inside, through and around the Capitol grounds. (This is a remote survey, I've yet to physically walk the grounds to verify the reading - not that they'd allow it). Ants or hornets might gravitate to the energy of this site, but I shudder to imagine walking into such a contentious storm of agitated energies day after day to solve the country's problems, help the American people and uphold the constitution!

Can a Senator or Congressperson overcome the energy they are standing in day after day without becoming the effect of it? Can anyone rise above the energy radiating from their environment? How long of an immersement can people endure before they become the energy? When is it time to move?

All these surveys and experiences have steered me to look at power with new eyes. How the human need for power and self importance imbalances the energy atmosphere of a place, draining the life force. Power corrupts indeed. Even on a small scale. For example, while surveying an elementary school I find a spot of old bully energy occupying the turf of the playground!

It stands to reason, metaphysically speaking, that our memory plays a role in reinforcing the energy of a place in time. Places in our childhood or recent past that still vibrate within us with pleasant or unpleasant feelings. Which raises questions about the resonant aspect of unreleased trauma and pain.

Is the energy of a place reinforced by our painful or happy memories of it? When one recalls a traumatic experience that occurred at a certain place, is the energy of the site touched by the memory in present time?

I've been sharing a number of experiences from sites I've surveyed that radiate unhealthy vibes. This is not always the case. Surveying a house in the Lake of the Isles district of Minneapolis, I'm surprised to discover a predominance of beneficial energy in the home. While the houses on either side carry a mix of neutral and detrimental energy.

Like many of the homes in the neighborhood, this three-story Victorian house had been built prior to the turn of the 20th century. Walking the property I pick up two bands of beneficial energy strong enough to keep at bay the incoming unhealthy currents. One runs east to west down the driveway between houses on the adjacent blocks. The other line runs North to South at the front door, which appears strong enough to neutralize the imbalanced line entering the property at the front walkway.

Physically the structure is sound and shows a history of upkeep. Some of the rooms in the house need a tune up, but overall, the house carries good vibes. The owner, a doctor who has lived in the home for twenty years, is familiar with its history. She shares how the previous two owners lived full lives and raised loving families.

The house requires some landscaping treatments to strengthen its borders, but overall, the home stands in good shape. Which speaks to the quality of energy emitted by its previous occupants. I'm sure if the walls could talk they'd recount the caring nature of the inhabitants. The families created an island of lasting good vibes in an urban setting, and the torch has been passed to a sensitive, space-conscious doctor who maintains it.

Caring goes a long way in creating a field of good vibes. Then again, you can be a caring individual and not be sensitive or conscious of the disturbed energy radiating from an underground fissure or water vein under your feet. Or you can be unaware of the energy you instill in a house that holds you there when you're attempting to move on.

Realtors scratch their heads over what to do with houses that refuse to sell. No matter how the place has been upgraded for curb appeal, how well it's staged for house hunters with the scent of home-baked bread wafting through the rooms, or how many times the price is reduced. Like everything, there can be a buffet of reasons, not all of them visible. In some instances the resistance is on a more subtle level. Potential buyers simply don't feel welcome or at ease in the house and when asked, they simply might not have the words to describe it. "It's not for us," or, "It doesn't feel right."

There are also houses that resist selling for other reasons.

I'm hired to survey a house that's been on the market for eight months.

The homeowners are at their wits end – hence the call. The house is clean, furnished, uncluttered and is located in an upscale neighborhood. Although the property has some energy issues, they are not serious enough to make one feel ill at ease. Yet there is something in the house I cannot at first get a handle on that may be a factor in its inability to sell.

As the homeowner walks me through the empty rooms, my attention is pulled to all the memories in the home of the family growing up. All the remodeling work and caring that went into it over the years. Stopping for a moment to listen to the house I begin to feel a low grade anxiety. Like the house is holding its breath.

I refuse to believe that the house has a mind of its own. Nor do I sense a possessive level holding on to the house. Could it be that the owners have not formally or completely, as a family, pulled their energy out and let go in a way that the house is open to someone new entering its domain?

I encourage the owners to conduct a letting go party. To go room to room in the spirit of gratitude and celebration, thanking the house for being a great home for them all those years, removing any anxieties about its future or their future, so that it may now be open to receive new ownership. Which gives new meaning to 'open house.'

Willing to try anything at this point, the homeowners make the rounds through the house, giving thanks, sharing their new life in another house, bringing everything to present time as they wish for the house to become a home for another person or family.

After months and months of sitting vacant with no interested buyers, within a week of conducting a conscious room by room letting go celebration, the house sells!

With so many energy characteristics and expressions, finding the applicable solution, correction or equation can take a few appearances and queries. Is it this? Is it that? The answer is not always immediately forthcoming. And on occasion, probing to determine the source or the affliction and method of treatment can be like waking up a sleeping monster.

ON THE ATTACK

Talk about naïve. When I first set out to do energy work I held the belief that ultimately everything seeks balance. Every life form, every being in its heart of hearts ultimately reaches for balance, connection and harmony. Maybe today it's feeling hurt and wants to hurt back, but this will pass.

Sure, it's acting excessively vengeful this minute, but give it time. Okay, it's out for blood right now, but ultimately it will come around. Afterall, Time, it is said, heals. And, isn't 'ultimately' way out there at the edge-tip of time?

What a revelation when I discover this is far from true. Not by a gazillion miles.

I'm checking out a commercial building. Running through the lobby is a hostile energy that brings an ache to my head as I crisscross through its field. I'd earlier discovered – the hard way - that there's a difference between disturbed energy and energy that's out to get you. Generally speaking, disturbed energy is like chaotic noise or radio static. It may be out of whack, unsteady, and unhealthy for people, but it's not out to attack you. You're simply standing in its field of imbalance. Then there's the more deliberate, malevolent, energy. This particular energy I speak of has attached itself to a meridian and is rampaging straight through the front door and out the back of the building intent on harming every living thing in its path.

As I walk the line, a voice pops in my ears, "Get Out!" This is odd because there's no one else around. I don't typically hear disembodied voices, yet this one pierces the veil. The shout repeats again only louder, "Get out of here!" A punishing voice; in English, no less. So intense, a wave of goose bumps stiffen the hairs on my arms. I take a step back, out of its line of fire.

Exploring the energy further, I determine the cause is a curse, an old curse originating near the site of the building. This curse energy is riding the meridian wielding the etheric equivalent of a sledge hammer. Curses are forever. One doesn't typically set a timer on a curse. It's invoked until the end of days.

Lesson learned. There are forces that are set on doing harm. Not connect. Not blend. Not seek balance. Not one good thing. A curse is just one of these forces. Another can stem from politically justified intent.

OF MISSILES AND MEN

I'm surveying a home situated close to the geographic center of the United States with a 360 view of the horizon. It is the site of a once active ICBM military base complete with command center and missile launch bunker. The installation was active in the early 60's with the military personnel on alert, performing drills during the Cuba missile crisis.

After walking around the periphery of the land and getting a sense of the outlying energies, Mitch, the enterprising homeowner, gives me a tour of the underground command center and launch bunker. Over the years, Mitch has renovated the command center into a completely furnished home and part of the bunker into a workspace.

I enter the launch bunker with a picture in my mind of a silo type shaft where the missile would lodge. Afterall they call them missile silos, don't they? No silo. The missile, long ago removed, had laid on its side, the thick steel roof would slide open (straight out of an old James Bond movie) and the missile would rise by an erector crane-like mechanism.

We're walking into the darker recesses of the bunker. Mitch is describing his vision of turning the place into a Peace Cathedral of healing and prayer when suddenly a force slams me with a wallop and I backpeddle away pointing to the source of the energy. Mitch says that's where the missile stood erect. He proceeds to push away a thick steel plate in the floor to reveal a deep blast cavity underneath.

"No!," I wave at him to high-tail it out of there. I check my clipboard to look at the map survey

I'd previously conducted of the launch building. Sure enough, the spiraling energy spot I'd marked on the drawing is where the missile once stood erect. I show it to Mitch and ask about the current of force I'd also noted on the drawing with a dotted line coming into this spiral spot from the side. He steps over to an opening in the concrete wall and points to an adjacent room where at one time a liquid oxygen tank stood with a pipe feed leading from it to the missile.

The experience moved me to look at the difference between warrior energy and warfare energy. Although their purpose may be similar, that of defense of home and land, the character of their energies is different. Warrior energy is honest, compassionate and clear. Its purpose is more about sustaining the life force than killing it. Yes, it will defend its freedom, its land, its family and community. To the death if necessary. However, it does not seek to harm children and innocent people. Nor does it react out of anger or vengeance. Yet way out here among the rolling plains smack dab in the middle of America that warrior energy has become entangled in politics, fear, anti-communism, and a weapon of mass destruction.

I share with Mitch how this intentional warfare energy has dug into the land as deep as the bunker and as wide as the barbed boundary wire. He may be able to calm the energy with prayer ceremonies, but every time there's a new military alert, or a threat, or talk of bombing another country, guess what — this bunker in the boonies begins to resonate to the old energy again, it's father's energy and intent, and the ghost missile rises up radiating its force-field of mass-murder.

INVISIBLE HARM, INVISIBLE HARMONY

A momentary summing up. Before I began exploring invisible energies I went about my life oblivious to the profound sensitivity of the Earth's energy field. Certainly aware of the harmful consequences stemming from physical acts of combat and violence, the pollution we proliferate, and our emotional effect on each other through interpersonal interaction, I had no idea how seemingly innocuous thought forms, intentions, emotions, caring, compassion, lies, apathy, and deceptive undertakings are absorbed into the living veins of the Earth and recycled back into our lives like a boomerang.

Whether harmful or harmonic, Time does not melt or clear the energy of our actions and emotions by itself. One doesn't have to experience past-life regressions to realize what has happened in previous times. Much of it is still here, emanating from the land, blowing the energy of past events up our legs and back in our face.

Then there's the realization of how the law of attraction plays out in the spirit of a place. How the energy of the site is affecting future happenings there. Unless cleared or transformed the harm or neglect that once transpired there can attract the same, or worse.

Another revelation comes from seeing how the energy released is not limited to certain geographic areas, or tied to the place where the event occurred. The energy is spread overland by the winds, conveyed along the geomantic meridians of the Earth, and by us. Round and round it goes. In the air we breathe. In the blood that circulates through our bodies. Although once invisible, it is made visible through our present actions, creations and the energy we emit.

Heraclitus once said, "Character is fate." Who you are frames your destiny. One could also say, "Energy is fate." And since everything is connected, collective energy frames collective destiny. In the character of energy radiating from the planet lies the future of mankind.

So, how does one begin to qualify the character of these invisible energies?

If you cannot sense it with your body, how do you determine if the land is radiating a harmful or harmonic energy?

What contributes to the energy that sacred sites emanate? And how can this energy be renewed or infused in the land and amplified in our lives?

7

DIVINING THE DIVINE

Locating Earth meridians with a pendulum is one thing. Qualifying the character and attributes of these emanations adds another dimension to the adventure.

Deciphering the qualities attributed to different subtle energy vibrations began to be cultivated through the study of radiesthesia. Allow me to speed through a haiku-short history of its vintage.

Circa the turn of the 20th century, the art of dowsing is taking root in parts of Europe and Great Britain. No longer limited to finding sources of subterranean water and precious metals, dowsing is now being utilized to search for all kinds of things - lost objects, lost people, criminals, archeological treasures, and cures for disease. Along comes a French Catholic priest and gifted dowser by the name Abbe Alexis Bouly who coins the term 'radiesthesia' to describe a field of study dedicated to the sensing by the human organism of rays and vibrations- radia (rays), thesia (perception). Individuals and groups gather under the umbrella of radiesthesia. Yet, lacking a unified inventory of detection systems which employs identical instruments and methods that achieve repeatable results weakens the credibility of radiesthesia as a viable means of accessing information beyond the five senses. At the crux of these mixed reviews is the distinction between the practitioners who operate from a mental perspective and those strictly studying the physical or vibratory plane.

MENTAL RADIESTHESIA

Mental radiesthesia works on a more psychic level. The practitioner is asking questions about decisions and choices in their lives or another's and applies a code or meaning to the responses he or she receives. Some people swear by the yes or no answers they obtain, and direct their lives around this technique. The validity of the answers depends on the receptor and the clarity of their source or field of information. Tricky stuff. Few, if any, can cleanly separate from personal experience, biases, beliefs, and desires which can color a reading. So, the slightest projection, assumption or prejudice will tilt the response of the practitioner's search.

PHYSICAL RADIESTHESIA

Physical, or vibratory radiesthesia, takes a scientific approach. Here the focus of attention is strictly on the waves and vibrations radiating from the object, or person, thus bypassing the subconscious mind, ego, and the personal associations of the practitioner. In this way one's energy field serves solely as an antenna to receive the subtle physical vibrations of the subject. The interaction is between the energy body of the practitioner and the vibrations emitted from the source of his or her attention. The 'psychic' ability and mental involvement of the practitioner is not activated, only the receptivity of the energy body is engaged.

While most practitioners during this time gravitated toward the mental side of radiesthesia, there were some intrepid explorers of the physical or vibratory forces at work. One such practitioner was another French Priest by the name of Abbe Mermet who made a thorough study of the rays emitted from various elements with the use of a pendulum.

Mermet's work included teleradiesthesia, or detection from a distance. Teleradiesthesia busts through the fourth wall, taking us into a dimension where physical distance is not a barrier. One can receive information about a subject miles away from the comfort of their lawn chair by using a representation of the distant place such as a topographical map, a plat, or an aerial photograph. This works through the law of similars. The map or picture is a sample of the actual physical place and therefore reflects vibratory information through matching resonance.

CHAUMERY & deBELIZAL

In the 1940's and 1950's, two French radiesthesiasts, Leon Chaumery and Antoine de Belizal, pioneered methods for detecting a spectrum of invisible energies and their qualitative effects on the human energy system. They named their science microvibratory physics.

Together, Chaumery and deBelizal created and employed many calibrated instruments to measure energy qualities. One of tools they invented is the virtual cone pendulum, a wonderfully simple energy quality detector. The pendulum consists of a disk that slides vertically up and down a straight shaft. By virtue of the geometric angles created between the edge of the disk and point of the shaft a number of frequencies become detectable by the operator. Much like a beam of clear light striking a prism branches into a rainbow of colors, the virtual cone pendulum identifies invisible radiations in a spectrum of vibratory frequencies. The frequencies include colors in the visible spectrum – red, green, blue, orange, yellow, indigo, and violet, and those from the invisible spectrum – ultra violet, infra-red, white, black and an energy ray that resides between black and white called Negative Green.

For evaluating radiations, the virtual cone pendulum is like a flashlight in the dark. It provides a simplified language for translating subtle energy emissions into qualities.

THE SHAPES OF THINGS

Using the virtual cone pendulum along with other detection devices, Chaumery and deBelizal were able to qualify vibrations from shapes, or shape-caused waves. These are measurable energy vibrations emanating from spheres, domes, pyramids, hemispheres and angles. The two explored and catalogued the emissions various shapes radiate, in combinations and in repetition, and the beneficial or toxic affect these waves have on the human organism.

Instruments for detecting and measuring subtle energies from shape-caused waves is not a recent invention. The Chinese ba-gua goes back thousands of years, as do pendulums found in sarcophagi from ancient Egypt. In fact the Egyptians were highly energy conscious as evidenced in their art and architecture. Form supplied a radiant function. The proportion and shape of their temples and statues were designed with energy transmission in mind. Each angle of their symbols and hieroglyphs were fastidiously calculated to emit intentional vibrations.

Chaumery and deBelizal examined the work of the Egyptians, amazed at their awareness of natural invisible forces and their mastery at producing enlivening, as well as dehydrating vibratory emissions though shape and symbol. Chaumery and deBelizal also developed various emitters engineered and tested to manifest specific subtle energy radiations. These emitters were made from shapes and symbols. They were not wired to an electrical source, plugged into a wall socket, or hooked to a battery. Simply shapes.

CASUALTIES OF EXPLORATION

Explorers of unknown worlds are highly susceptible to accidents and misfortunes. In 1957 Leon Chaumery passed away as a result of his exposure to a particular band of highly noxious energy. It has also been sited that Enel, a radiesthesia practitioner in Egypt who worked with the virtual cone and universal pendulums, went the way of Chaumery, his death attributed to detrimental energies he contacted in his healing work.

The prolific and foundational microvibrational research work of these scientists and other radiesthesia practitioners did not go for nought. The baton passed on to an Egyptian architect.

DR. IBRAHIM KARIM

While working for the Ministry of Health in Egypt, Dr. Karim met two doctors who were associated with a school of radiesthesia based on Enel's works. Ibrahim's interest in physical radiesthesia became ignited the day one of the doctors showed him a virtual cone pendulum. Dr. Karim had studied color systems as an architecture student in Zurich, and upon seeing the pendulum he instantly envisioned prismatic colors radiating out from it.

Later, while on assignment in Paris, Dr. Karim took time to visit the Radiesthesia Center there. He was searching for any materials he could get his hands on that would help further illuminate the vibratory physics of radiesthesia, only to discover that the Center was dedicated to the psychic or mental side of radiesthesia. Dr. Karim's search appeared to be in vain, until an older woman at the Center overheard his inquiries. When he told her he was an Egyptian architect interested in physical radiesthesia, the woman replied, "You're finally here!" She trundled down some stairs and brought back a passel of dusty books by Chaumery and deBelizal, whom she'd personally known, along with their instruments. Karim informed her that he didn't have the money to pay for the materials. The woman didn't flinch and freely gave him the books and instruments, saying they belonged to him. Since that day, vibratory radiesthesia became his path and passion of study. Little did Dr. Karim know at the time that one day he would be carrying out Chaumery and deBelizal's deepest wish for vibratory radiesthesia to become a full-fledged science.

Being an architect, Dr. Karim could directly apply the work of Chaumery and deBelizal to his designs, exploring the ways shape-caused waves affect the state of energy radiating from the structures we build and the sites where we build them.

Living in Egypt, everywhere Dr. Karim turned stood fantastic temples, obelisks, pyramids and tombs precisely fashioned and placed with absolute precision to amplify specific invisible energies. An open laboratory and library at his doorstep, where he could re-discover the ancient spiritual science of energetic architecture unrealized for ages. It was the perfect landscape to explore and to question, 'What is shape? What is energy? Is there a geometrical way of transmitting the wisdom of Nature through shape and architecture? Why not use qualitative scales for building instead of quantitative scales? And, how to create a design language, a language of quality that brings about balance and vitality - a transcendental language, archetypal in nature, working with natural laws, one written by wisdom, not intellect.

At a time when science directed its endeavors toward quantitative measurements and results, Dr. Karim begins applying scientific methods to the physics of energy qualities. A revolutionary science that works in harmony with Nature to bring about healing to an imbalanced world through the inter-relationship of shapes, sounds, symbols, colors and numbers. An architecture that heals.

According to Dr. Karim, architecture is the domain of healing. Whereas treatment and repair is the function of the medical establishment. But there is one underlying problem with contemporary architecture - it is missing the energy component. It is missing the consciousness of radiance that his Egyptian ancestors employed. Buildings today neither connect to the Earth nor to people in a holistic and harmonic way. The vibrations they emit are so unattached and out of tune with natural balancing forces that merely being inside their walls can be a drain on the organism.

Since an architect is a sculptor of space, how can one create living spaces that are human-friendly? Spaces designed to help balance the energy fields of those within it through invisible shape-caused waves? And what are these energies?

SACRED SITE ENERGY QUALITIES

During his many years of research, Dr. Karim found three highly beneficial energies common to sacred sites that can be detected using the virtual cone pendulum - Horizontal Negative Green, a Higher Harmonic of Ultra-Violet, and a Higher Harmonic of Gold.

Horizontal Negative Green is the magnetic waveform of the Negative Green carrier wave discovered by Chaumery and deBelizal. Horizontal Negative Green is an energy quality that can be found emanating where two different surfaces meet, and can be felt along ocean shorelines and the banks of streams. While the horizontal aspect of Negative Green is beneficial, the vertical aspect, or electric waveform of the Negative Green carrier wave is highly toxic to the human organism. It is this unhealthy energy that contributed to Chaumery's death.

A Higher Harmonic of Ultra Violet is another energy quality common to sacred sites. It is also known as the angelic ray and in spiritual traditions this energy helps join one with the angelic realm that acts on divine will and brings with it a calming and enlivening radiation. Dr. Karim found this Ultra Violet quality emanating from people in prayer. He also perceived an increase in this energy in the atmosphere at dawn and at sunset - the pivoting times.

The third energy Dr. Karim discovered to be common to sacred sites is a Higher Harmonic of Gold – like the illuminated gold one sees in the auras of saints depicted in religious icon paintings. The energy carries a divine vitality and can also be detected at the center of a circle or sphere, however small or large the size of the circle or sphere may be. This harmonic of Gold relates to physical gold only at a higher octave or vibratory rate. (*)

Dr. Karim found that when these three energies - the Higher Harmonic of Gold, a Higher Harmonic of Ultra Violet and Horizontal Negative Green are produced at a site or in the field of a living body, they bring about a state of welcome balance.

Using geometry as a basis, Dr. Karim began to assemble a design language that brings balance to living organisms by reproducing the three qualities of energy found at sacred sites. Dr. Karim's studies in the physics of quality became the seed for a new science, which he founded in 1992.

BIOGEOMETRY

This new science, BioGeometry, is dedicated to the study and application of shapes for harmonizing energy fields. The science seeks to organize a holistic geometry of spirit that infuses the environment with the three energies found at sacred sites in order to balance and support living organisms.

For Dr. Karim it is, "...like widening the window we are looking through to include all that is invisible at this moment. The paranormal becomes part of the normal and spirituality becomes part of science."

Not wishing his new science of BioGeometry to become a fad like so many other trends in architecture, Dr. Karim decided to only take on projects that would further his research. Projects that would give BioGeometry a solid scientific footing.

Along with his architectural designs, Dr. Karim has created a number of BioGeometry instruments designed to access the three sacred radiations and transform the energy of a space. Some instruments work to bring balance to Earth meridians, some help to harmonize interiors, while other instruments are intended to minimize the unhealthy effects of electromagnetic fields on the human organism.

Dr. Karim is acutely aware of the hidden time bomb of the information age and how the electromagnetic waves being created by our technology is harming our immune system on a collective level.

"The age of information brings with it the extinction of life. It has produced electronic carrier waves in the atmosphere. The wonderful flair of the information society will bring us to the threshold where the immune system collapses – human, animal and plant."

During lunch at one of his workshops, Dr. Karim shares a wonderful story that vividly illustrates the application of his BioGeometry instruments and shapes to remedy the debilitating effects of the electromagnetic fields in the village of Hemberg, Switzerland.

SWISS STORY

Soon after the installation of a Swisscom mobile communications antenna in the tower of the Hemberg church, villagers suddenly and inexplicably begin suffering migraines, fatigue, dizziness, sleeplessness, ringing in the ears, and depression. Their precious cattle start having miscarriages. Plants wither before their eyes. Songbirds and bats suddenly vanish from the area and do not return.

Villagers feel smothered by what they believe to be the negative radiation transmitting from the new antenna in the church. Gathering together, a group of Hemberg families take their grievances to Swisscom and to the Swiss Government. Time passes. Nothing improves. Tensions escalate. The once peaceful hamlet becomes polarized with frustration and rage.

After a year of protesting to Swisscom and the Swiss government, word reaches Dr. Karim in Cairo. Dr. Karim is no stranger to Switzerland having received his doctorate in Zurich. Dr. Karim arrives in Hemberg with his toolbox of shapes, pendants, symbols and odd-looking wood and plastic forms. He is faced with two challenges - that of transforming the harmful radiations, and that of gaining the confidence of a village of stern and irritable people not inclined to open up to strangers readily, if at all. News of his coming creates cynical doubts. Some think he is a puppet for Swisscom. The environmentalists are just as suspicious and believe he is part of a government plot. Others, seeing the short, stocky sixty-year-old man walking about the village dangling a brass pendulum from his fingers, are certain he is a charlatan.

Dr. Karim installs his BioGeometrical shapes in the church tower. He attaches numerically notched plastic strips on electrical wires and symbols on the main electrical panel. He fastens large wooden and plastic forms that look like oversized chess pieces in precise locations around the town and in the homes of affected residents.

Within a week the health of those afflicted improves, and the emotional climate and quality of life in Hemberg transforms as the negative energy fields are harmonized. The villagers are amazed and delighted by the Egyptian's seemingly miraculous achievement. But not everyone is satisfied, or believes it to be true. There are still a few stubborn skeptics who think it's all hocus-pocus, that Swisscom decreased the wattage, or that Dr. Karim is a hypnotist who through some mode of autosuggestion entranced the village. Yet, if this is the case, how does it explain the songbirds and bats returning to Hemberg? The plants now growing profusely? And the cattle birthing healthy calves once again?

Today, more and more Swiss are asking Dr. Karim to employ his BioGeometry magic to their towns and villages. And he continues to develop innovative tools, instruments and methods to help harmonize spaces and assist in the curing of disease.

Raising and nurturing a new born science, especially one based on expanding human awareness of invisible vibrations, is no small task! Yet Dr. Karim believes, "Only those who can see the invisible can do the impossible."

8

EYES OF A SEER

I'm trying to keep up with Donna Fortune as she veers sharply from the scraggily field we had just been looking at and heads off into a woodland area. There's no trail to speak of. Ambling along, her mother bear of a body lifts one leg over a fallen maple tree. "Next life I'm going to be slim and tall with long legs," she states with fierce insistence.

Donna is a rare being - a direct-control, physical trance medium (*), Earth intuitive, and grandmother, who I've been fortunate to know for 25 years. There are psychics and clairvoyants and then there's Donna. In olden times she'd be adorned with the title of 'oracle.' In today's new age nomenclature she's called a channel. And channel she does. Donna brings voice to an ocean of beings, centrally 'The Teacher', a teacher of souls. Donna is also a great teacher in her own right. Her body carries an extraordinary range of awareness. Every place she steps she can describe the energy or spirit of the site. She can look at an old painting or sculpture and know the emotion the artist was feeling at the time of its creation. The reach and scope of her perception appears boundless and continues to grow, whether it's peering deep into the crust of the planet and sharing its geophysical makeup, or trotting through time dimensions to determine when a particular event occurred.

Today we're exploring an area I'd found to be severely troubled, a ragged energy I couldn't get a clear reading on.

"Oh, this is yucky," she says, half-smiling.

I'm trailing behind her with my wife, Veronica, and kindred spirits, Michael and Tricia Maley in tow. We're chatting along when Donna abruptly stops. "Don't come any further," she warns. "Not yet." She takes a few more steps. "They're attacking me."

"Who's attacking you?"

"Oh, this is annoying." Which is Donna's way of saying the beings or energies inhabiting the site are attempting to do her in. So, we wait, watching her press on through the woods, knowing she's working to get a bead on who or what these hostile forces are.

Although I speak of Donna with wonder and appreciation, I often take her gifts for granted. Then there are times like this where her willingness and ability at confronting evil energies comes into play and I'm touched with awe once again.

"They separated the land from the Earth," she calls back to us.

"They what?"

"People here, long, long time ago. Not white people. Not native Americans. Before that. They actually separated this land right here from the Earth."

I don't have a clue what she means. Looking around you'd think everything was fine. The trees don't really show visible signs of disease or dark forces. They aren't exactly resplendent with life either. And for a woodland, there's a notable lack of bird song. In fact, the more I open up to the surrounding energy field the more I sense a silent deadness in the air, followed by a low grade apprehension that ripples through my body.

"Okay, you can come now," she beckons us on, having cleared the way. We follow her toward a small, dark spindly tree growing at the center of the energy.

"You want evil. This is pure evil."

Shortly after working to clear the area of dark energies, we hear the chirping of birds in the trees above our heads.

Donna later explains, "Whenever you take the sound of life from the land, whether animal or human, the land breaks. You break the balance of nature and the land becomes separated from the Earth."

The land can also be broken where there is extensive clear cutting of old growth trees. While surveying a plat of a residential property I picked up a loss or lack of a highly valuable energy that had been removed at one time from the land. I didn't know what to attribute it to – an excavation of minerals or crystals? I only knew the source carried great intrinsic value. Later that day, walking the site with Donna, she saw how the underground fungus layer had been destroyed. This unsung fungus layer is a vital, foundational organ in the life of a forest. A casualty of strip-logging the old maple, oak and basswood 'Big Woods' of Minnesota was the destruction of this fungus layer and with it much of the life force in the land.

My experiences working and traveling with Donna could fill volumes. For this manuscript I'll confine it to particular gems of knowledge she's taught me during this year in the field that relate to the energy work I'd undertaken.

What follows are some cut-to-the-chase outings with Donna where she pointed out energies and dimensional states I'd previously been unaware. Her uncanny observations have been extremely helpful to me in clarifying and broadening the scope of my site surveys. It's doubtful I would ever be conscious of so many invisible radiations without her insight and guidance. These experiences may bust your boundaries of belief – but, hey, you've made it this far!

WHEN SHAMAN GO DARK

My friend Marc called me to check out a house with him near Lake Minnetonka. The lake, deemed sacred by the Dakota and Ojibwa nations, is actually a chain of large bays formed when the glaciers receded following the last ice age. In 1851 a treaty was drawn up to transfer ownership of the lake and 2 million acres of surrounding Native American land to the U.S. Government. Because of the lakes' spiritual significance and the many burial sites in the woodland mounds around its shores, a request to keep the lake in tribal hands was proposed. The request was denied. Many of the chiefs refused to sign the government treaty. Nevertheless, the treaty was enforced.

Today the shoreline of the lake is studded with homes, fine homes, yet, looks can be deceiving. The homeowner who had called Marc had a bit of a problem. Disturbing things were happening in the house - hauntings, the tromping of feet going up and down the stairs in the night, ceiling lights exploding, the main electrical panel arcing. Things like that. The homeowner had previously called on a Feng Shui expert, then a ghost buster. Nothing much changed. Marc and I discovered a wide line of intensely rugged energy angling through the garage on through the kitchen and dining room. We also found a narrower agitated grid line running perpendicular through the stairway and intersecting the wide line inside the house directly above the main electrical panel located in the lower level.

When we asked about the neighborhood, the homeowner told us how in the past few years, two houses in the cul de sac caught fire and two different neighbors became stricken with cancer.

We called in Donna to determine the nature of the entities riding the line. She sat down in a chair in the lower level of the house near the intersection of primary disturbance and brought in one extremely pissed off shaman. After a barrage of aggressive venting, the shaman explained how he is one of many other shaman who had once lived around the lake and who were devoted to protecting the life of the water. Informing us how we had brutishly taken and poisoned these sacred lands and waters, the shaman confessed that in their anger, he and the other guardians had become dark and done some harm as well. In the end, they agreed to leave - leaving us with the colossal mess we've made. This is one instance in a number of areas around the lake where development has noticeably upset the residing guardian spirits.

Hearing the shaman speak his unvarnished truth, I couldn't help but wonder what life would be like if everyone could see and interact with the guardian spirits of the land and waters. Would we then center our attention on sustaining and even boosting the vitality of our natural surroundings? And would this be enough to fulfill the ambitions of our lives?

CHOLERA EPIDEMIC

Surveying a house in West St. Paul, I pick up a toxic level in the soil. I don't know what caused it. It feels old, perhaps a once active factory or a slaughter house. Bringing Donna to the site we learn that the land radiates the effects of an epidemic, more specifically, an outbreak of cholera in the area many years ago.

Cholera is a highly contagious disease, yet previous to coming to the home none of us were aware of such an epidemic in the area. With a bit of research we find that there were actually two outbreaks, one in 1852 and then another in 1866. Both are attributed to bacteria in the nearby Mississippi River.

This epidemic energy became imprinted in the land along the east bank of the river, and even after 150 years, it still bears a dulling effect on the vitality of the land.

One might ask, is the dulling of the energy in the land here due to the bacteria that may still be present, but not contagious? Or is it due to the sickness and death of the inhabitants? Or is it both?

BRICK & POROUS ROCK ABSORPTION

Surveying a home in Deephaven, I realize right away there's trouble. Pulling into the driveway the family dog approaches me slowly, cowering in utter surrender. *This is no watch dog, that's for sure.*

Walking the grounds my body crackles with oppositional energies, some geopathic and some peopathic - trauma, conflict, pain, fire, and who knows what else. I don't normally 'see' entities, but when a shadow figure extends his hands to me pleading for help, I reach for the phone and call Donna.

Besides the remnant energies of the site, Donna helps me see how some building materials such as brick, cement block and certain porous landscaping stones absorb and emit the energy originating or passing through the site. This includes fireplaces and patio pavers, as well as the brick walls of the structure itself. The difficulty comes in clearing these unhealthy energies from brick and porous stone without having to take them out or replace them altogether. One can treat the land around the house, but the energy is still locked in the brick and stone. I picture myself having to tell clients, 'The energy around your home has been balanced. Now, there's just this one last little thing you need to do -

dismantle your fireplace and remove all the brick exterior walls.'

On the plus side, porous stone can be used in certain applications to soak up toxins in the ground, as long as the stone is later taken out and pulverized.

I SMELL SULFUR

In 2004 tens of thousands of adult white pelicans suddenly fled the Chase Lake Wildlife Refuge in North Dakota, abandoning their nests and leaving their chicks and eggs to die. Being one of the largest habitats for white pelicans in the country with more than 35,000 birds counted at one time, this remains a baffling incident.

The following year a group of us venture north to the refuge with Donna to see if we can determine the cause and, if possible, to help restore balance to the area so that the white pelicans might return to their long standing nests.

An icy wind blows in our faces as we trudge around the desolate and foreboding shoreline of the lake. At one point Donna stops and says, "I smell sulfur." She brings in the energy of the place and we learn how a lava dome is forming underground beneath the area. Why is this happening here?

To understand the reason one needs to realize how our oil and natural gas drilling, along with the depletion of underground aquifers impacts the tender balance of the Earth's crust. Subterranean reservoirs, oil, and natural gas serve as the lubricant and cooling fluid of the planet. They work to keep it flexible and in relative equilibrium. By extracting what we call our natural resources, cracks and cavities develop. These cracks allow deeper molten energies to rise and over time a volcano or caldera can surface. Miles to the west and north of the refuge, oil and natural gas drilling is underway. The smell of sulfur can be an indication of volcanic activity. It can also be a reason why the white pelicans deserted their nests.

Depleting aquifers, the large underground reserves of water can also create a seismic imbalance, as well as impact the local climate. Water resonates to water. Rain falls more where groundwater exists, than where no groundwater exists.

AS BELOW, SO ABOVE
Scientists are well aware of natural cataclysms causing extinction of species at various times throughout the history of the planet from such dramatic events as asteroid collisions with the Earth, volcanic ash clouds blocking the sun for years, and cold snaps that blanket the globe in ice. It's important to know that although the extinction may have been of natural origin, these sites where the extinction took place may still radiate the energy not only from the land but also through the vegetation and bodies of those inhabiting the area for extended periods of time.

This became evident at one site where Donna and a group of us ventured. If you can picture rock strata – the layering of geological changes in the crust of the Earth – and view it through 'energy glasses', you can begin to see how deep under our feet there are also layers of traumatic events and upheavals that today apply an active pressure on the health and state of mind of those living above.

Walking the ground of the site where a past extinction took place, Donna bluntly pronounces, "People should not be living here."

I previously noted the deteriorating influence underground streams and fissures and faults can have on human health. Centers of extinction energy can likewise be extremely harmful and draining to a body. Perhaps a saint might be able to cope with the energy, but realistically, depending on a person's condition, character and the length of exposure, they could become deathly sick and/or become a walking contagion of the energy, discharging it through harsh, uncaring words and divisive behavior wherever they go. The energy is no longer fixed to the site, but is carried outward by those who have absorbed it. We are, afterall, hosts of our habitat. There's a saying, "If you wish to know the character of the people, look at the energy of the land they inhabit."

DOORWAYS

On numerous woodland outings we would encounter invisible doorways between two or more trees. Donna describes them as both physical and etheric multi-dimensional connections to the solar system. Our solar system also has doorways that connect to the galaxy, and so on.

These Earth-based doorways are portals where we can touch the solar system. However, to pass through a doorway is no simple feat. Like a combination lock, each doorway has an energy equation. This equation is the key. To pass through a doorway you need to consciously match the energy of the doorway by radiating the same vibratory level with your body. At each doorway stand one or two souls, or doorway guardians. When asked about these guardians, Donna described them as old Light Beings who have protected these doorways since the time when humans became dense and dark (which is a whole other story). If a person is able to match the energetic equation they can then pass through the doorway, and when they do, more souls come to greet them on the other side. These souls can help people with what they may need at the time.

Once you manage to pass through a doorway the equation for that doorway changes. "Nothing stays the same," Donna says, "The equations are constantly changing," adding, "If I don't grow, I can't go through it again."

81

There are also false doorways. Places that look like they may be a doorway, but are intended to throw you off.

"It's always a test," Donna says, "...a test of your consciousness. And the unwillingness to seek consciousness borders on neglect."

Trouble is, people are unconsciously walking through these invisible doorways all the time without knowing or sensing they exist. I know I have. And, every time this happens, I don't receive any energy, and I miss the opportunity of connecting to an expanded level of self.

Noticing how most of the doorways we've encountered are located on Earth meridians, I ask Donna about what I call sky beams, columns of energy I've bumped into that rise from the ground out into space.

"Those are doorways."

"What about in cities and towns? Are there doorways present there?"

"No, the asphalt and concrete eliminate them. We've lost a lot of doorways."

LAND HEALING

"Ta-ta-ta-ta-ta-ta... ta-ta-ta-ta-ta-ta..." Donna is chanting a rhythmic tune as she struts through an area of detrimental energy. Her hiking shoes tap to the beat of her ditty on the forest path, "Ta-ta-ta-ta-ta-ta... ta-ta-ta-ta-ta-ta." Her glee is purposeful. She is expressing her sound with joy – an energy that's utterly absent from the place.

"I work to bring in more dimensions," she explains. "I look to see where the predator energy is, and what energy I can bring to the area the predator won't go to."

In this place, she's trying to raise the vibratory level by going into a playful mode that introduces more life and more dimensions. She first connects to her heartbeat and brings out her sound amidst all the other sounds.

"And then you'll notice, I'll change my sound. I'll match it and bring lively energy to it with my sound and my movement, and then I'll keep changing my sound."

Donna works on healing a site in multiple ways. All of which give new meaning to the phrase, 'working the land.'

"You have to first really know what the Earth needs. You have to be able to hear what sound it is saying. You have to be able to hear the tone of the sound. Now usually, if it's really traumatized, there's only one tone. Very little dimension. So you'd be in a place without many dimensions. That would be the first thing you would notice about it. The solidity of the place. And the non-functioning of the place. And even though there might be a stream of water, plants and birds, there would typically be fewer. And more often than not, what you get there is an over abundance of animals of prey."

Color is another valuable mode of healing for Donna. Depending on the site, she may begin by embodying a high vibratory radiance of what she calls, 'the Light of Life.' and immediately, as if by magnetic attraction, the spectrum of color rays come to this light. Donna describes this "Light of Life" as the light of the sun combined with the fire of the Earth together. Light follows sound. Color follows light. Where there's a lack of sound, you'll find a lack of light and color.

Depending on the site, and the degree of severity, Donna may seek a source of healing and transformation from down under. She does this by directing her consciousness into the Earth below her feet. Her intention is to find the broken place, the center of the harm, and then go beyond it to find true healthy energy, however deep that may be, which sometimes can be miles down. Once found, with its agreement, she brings it to the surface to heal the land. The source of the healthy energy can be subterranean crystals, gemstones, a spring or body of pure water, even a geological formation or pre-ancient asteroid remnant that was involved in the birth of the planet. Donna's search for a level of multi-dimensional aliveness is not instantaneous. Some areas take a bit of exploration, mining the depths.

Once she locates a healthy energy, she connects with it, and with its cooperation, she assists in bringing the energy to the surface to heal the existing energy of the land. Nothing is forced or coerced. She extends this healthy energy as deep and as wide as she can. Of course it helps to be conscious of what healthy energy feels like and to know if it is appropriate to the place at this time.

"A person may think they're doing good, but, what's good or evil to the land is different than what you may think. Most people don't know how to bring balance with nature's laws. How we heal must always be with nature's laws. One must let go of all ego, expectations and what you believe to be right or wrong."

This is not something I recommend anyone try for themselves. Donna is an exceptional being who is highly skilled in this interaction.

JUST SAY HELLO

I'm driving Donna up and down streets around St. Louis Park, an older suburb situated a couple miles west of Minneapolis. We stop at various spots and walk around, scouting the prevailing land energies, all of which make us wince and moan. We know the cause - a now defunct tar factory once dumped toxic chemicals in the ground producing a plume which today extends some 8 square miles.

Donna had previously identified a cluster of giant, radiant crystal stones as old as time, buried a thousand feet deep in one part of the suburb. The stones are smothered, their animate life force unable to penetrate the layers of tarry yuck. Donna is looking at ways to open the land, clear the thick mantle of contamination so the energy of the stones may rise and restore health and vitality to the surrounding environs.

Having aspirations to become more adept at inter-dimensional communication I ask her, "How do you do it? How do you connect so well to the spirit of a place?"

"You simply say, 'hello'."

Stopping to inspect one site, I turn and stare at a strip of land alongside a walking path, cup my hands and shout, "Hello!"

"Do it again," she says. "Only this time drop all ego. Set yourself aside. Then say hello."

I know what she means, just not how to achieve it at the drop of a hat. What she means is stepping back from personal projections, agendas, intentions, and truly listening inside. Allow the land or the life form to express its experience either in sound, in pictures, in a body sensation or 'knowing'. To do this one must drop not only their ego, but also their control.

"Let go of the way things are supposed to be and be in the way things are. You cannot find truth in what is supposed to be, or what is fair."

Donna's unique intuitive gifts are not easily translatable into scientific measurement and methodology. Yet without the eyes of the seer, science would be without a torch light.

9

ENERGY REMEDIES

Whether by scientific method or through the eyes of a seer, it's evident that unhealthy energies can be detected and qualified. We have the tools at hand - radiesthesia instruments, muscle testing, and the intuitive sensitivities of our bodies. Now, how can we transform the energy so it's no longer harmful to us? How can we interact with the spirit of a place so that it is free of geopathic and peopathic contamination?

Allow me to share my working mode, a set of stages that evolved somewhat over the course of doing the work, and no doubt will evolve further. These stages are:

1. The Remote Survey
2. The Site Survey
3. Findings & Recommendations
4. Application of Energy Remedies
5. The Follow Up

THE REMOTE SURVEY

The Remote Survey is a preliminary charting of the site. In this initial stage a current map, aerial photo, plat or plan view of the home, clinic, office or property is surveyed remotely for influential energies, meridians, underground fissures and streams, along with other subterranean and historic influences.

Not only does this survey show the rough locations of primary beneficial and harmful global grid lines, one can also determine the quality and character of their emanations. Whether it is for an existing structure or raw land, conducting a remote survey can save the time and expense of traveling to the site and walking the entire grounds. I can learn a great deal about the energy of a place from an accurate representation of it at a distance. The more faithful the map, photo or drawing is in terms of compass points, proportion, topography and detail, the better it resonates with the actual physical place and more capable it is of rendering a clear account of the prevailing energies. Also, starting with the remote survey also distances the practitioner from resonating as intensely with the harmful forces that may be radiating from the site.

The Remote Survey is not something to trust fully and report your findings to the homeowners without first validating the information physically. As a rough blueprint, however, the findings continue to surprise me.

THE SITE SURVEY

With the Remote Survey in hand, I will make a physical survey of the site to verify the findings and to discover more. I will pinpoint the exact locations of the meridians and auspicious areas on the property, and further characterize their harmful and beneficial qualities in more detail. If needed, I will bring along associates and experts to give additional interpretations of the site — its geologic history, scientific data showing the existence of underground streams and fissures, past human activities, namely industrial, historic battles and early habitation.

Walking the site, I can better sense the amount of life force radiating from the land. The visual world comes into play as I observe the topography, interact with the trees, animals and insects - features I could not register as distinctly when conducting the remote survey. I can see what is happening in the vicinity, the neighborhood, industries and new developments located just beyond the site. I can also sense the presence or lack of nature spirit and deva activity, which is an essential component in the vitality of the land . This site survey also reinforces the intensities, the dominant direction of flows, the sources of disruption, and the places emanating life enriching energies.

FINDINGS & RECOMMENDATIONS

Before sharing the information I've gathered with the occupants or property owners, I'll ask them a series of fairly elaborate questions that shed light on their experience living there. These include their knowledge of the history of the site. Questions regarding their health and the health of neighbors. Are there places they tend to gravitate? Are there places or rooms they avoid? I find it better to interview the clients *after* I've completed surveying the property so I can be clear-minded in my initial search and not programmed to be looking for certain energies or areas they've named.

The occupant's experience can reveal a lot and provide answers and stories that support the energies I'm picking up, as well as other areas I may have overlooked. Depending on the people and the site I may invite them on a tour of their property to see if they sense the primary imbalances and places of harmonious energies. The tour may include checking how their body responds to certain places, muscle testing them so that they can physically experience the balanced and imbalanced energy radiations. What is interesting about the tour is how often things come up that they previously didn't speak about. Yet when I point out a particular area and the type of energy emanating from a spot, their awareness kicks in. 'You know, I never feel comfortable in that room.' Or, 'Oh that's right, that's where such and such happened.'

By now I've established what treatments to recommend. Along with my recommendations I make a point of letting the occupants know how, much like us, the land has a history that affects the way it connects to people. By highlighting the areas where the land has been harmed and neglected, or experienced hurtful human activity, these energies are bound to come out stronger. Once named, the energy amplifies. Sometimes it is instantaneous. I'll get a bead on a harsh energy emanating from a site and all of sudden it's spitting acid. I know it's not about me, but it may be about my species. A recoil of the way people have treated the land in the past.

APPLICATION OF ENERGY REMEDIES

With the occupant's blessing, I move on to the remedial work. Much like bodywork, energy work on the land may require successive treatments. Typically there's more than one area that needs to be treated on a property. In fact, there may be so many, it helps to work them in successive stages— broad stokes first, balance the major disturbances, then move layer after layer with finer and finer enhancements as occupant's interest and budget permits.

My preference in treating a property is to start outside and then move inside. First work to balance the unhealthy energies that are entering the property from the outer boundaries. By balancing these land energies first, the air is cleared to better assess the interior spaces.

One always needs to be careful about entering a site with an "I've come to heal you" attitude. This cocky energy rides the same bus as control and possession.

Best to question one's quest. Does the area wish to be healed? Am I the one capable of healing the land? Am I out of fear? Is this the best time for the good of all concerned? This last question is important because I may not be aware of hidden ramifications beyond my immediate perception.

STONE ENERGYSCAPING

Rocks continue to amaze me with what they're capable of doing when it comes to transforming the energy of a site. Being mindful of the type of stone, the number and the configuration, they can work marvels.

I'd once heard that river rocks could help balance disturbed Earth radiations. I experimented with them and became an instant believer. Obtaining them was another story. My initial tactic was to gather them myself. Why buy river rocks when they're right there in the water ripe for the plucking? I'd hike down riverbanks and along streams in the area, searching for likely candidates. I'd wade out into the water and dangle a pendulum over each rock until I picked up it's wavelength, then determine if it would be willing and able to balance a geopathic stress zone. If the pendulum spun in the affirmative, I'd heft the rock away and set it in the trunk of my car.

One afternoon, trudging in rubber boots through the rushes along Minnehaha Creek cradling a sizeable rock in one arm, I sunk up to my waist in muck. Hard as I twisted and torqued my body, I could not extricate myself. Every time I attempted to lift a leg, the mud would create a suction-lock around it. A voice in my head directed me to lose the rock and the boots. Instead, I stopped trying to hoist my legs free, and just slogged forward, forcing my body through the wall of muck by sheer will. Finally I managed to reach firmer ground. From that day on, I did my gathering at local rock and landscaping outlets that carry river rocks and other natural stone.

When shopping for capable stones I'll bring along a plat, aerial photo or scale drawing of the property to the rock yard, set it on the edge of a bin with the pendulum oscillating above it. My energy body serves as an open mediation tool registering compatibilities and incompatibilities. With my other hand I reach down and touch each rock to see if it is willing and able to energy balance this particular land. Surprising the number of rocks that indicate, "No."

Communicating to rocks may sound crazy, yet the more you work with them on an energy level, the more they talk back, with information expressed through vibration. Once you hear them, they were talking all along. Some stones are more conscious than others. The more conscious ones appear to enjoy having a purpose, appreciate connection and being given a voice in the matter.

Meeting with the owner of one rock outlet I shared the type of energy work I do and how I've found many stones to be conscious beings that need to be treated with more respect. He nodded and said, "I've come to a place in my life where I allow every person the right to his or her own beliefs."

The process of treating a site with rocks, or what I call stone energyscaping, plays out like this: Once I determine the primary agitated meridians, intersections or areas that need to be balanced, I then seek to establish the type of stone and its configuration that will be most effective.

ROCK CONFIGURATONS

There are a number of stone sets and layouts I employ. These include traditional corner stones, lines of stones, stone circles, and standing stones, plus a design of my collaboration, which I call the arrow and rudder configuration.

I say collaboration because the formation came about while treating a site with river rocks all the while being aware I was working with the assistance of the land devas. The configuration is basically a 45 degree (more or less) arrow or V shape of touching river rocks that point toward the incoming direction of the irritated energy current (s), with a single stone or rudder, placed inside the chevron.

The rocks are not simply set in formation. Each one has its own nesting place, which I determine by measuring for compatibilities. Rocks also have an upside and a downside. Sometimes you can feel this by holding them in your hands. In stone energyscaping, one must set aside personal attraction. Beauty is not always the determining factor in stone placement. In many cases, the more attractive side of a rock is turned toward the ground, and the more mottled, scarred, or bumpy side faces up, much to the disappointment of the homeowner. It's all about efficacy and not about looking good.

Rocks also respond to being oriented a certain way. So, once I have them temporarily set in position I turn each rock slowly until I receive the strongest energetic response. What never stops startling me is how the stones orient into each other so fittingly, like a jigsaw puzzle, with no control, agenda or influence on my part.

Is their upside and orientation based on where they were born, extruded, how they aligned with magnetic North, where they surfaced, or how they rolled out of the retreating glacier? Or is it how they will be most effective in transforming the energy, given the place and the configuration?

With the configuration in place, I then check to see if there's a shift in the radiant energy emitting from the meridian or area of imbalance. Typically the shift is instantaneous. Outside the configuration the readings will show no shift. As I pass over the point stone in the configuration, the energy becomes neutralized. Then, moving further across the rock configuration, the energy transforms to a healthier, more balanced emanation.

I've returned after a time and found that this rudder rock can be tweaked again and again to fine tune the strength of the stone design which can transform a meridian for quite a distance. Sometimes all it takes is pivoting the rudder a titch.

I once asked Justin, my geologist friend, "What makes river rocks so good at balancing certain disturbed earth energies?" He described how stone has magnetic particles in it. In a river, the force of the water washing over it will further magnetize the rocks. This magnetic energy must be what helps calm the agitation. Makes sense to me. And would it not also be the flowing energy pattern of the water, absorbed into the stone, smoothing and tumbling it against other stones. And with it, the sound. Wouldn't the sound of the water rushing and churning with such constant action be embodied as well?

I've also learned through Donna Fortune how water is highly effective in eradicating evil energies. It is so fluid, connective and enlivening, the rigid and dis-connective character of evil cannot exist in its field.

Crystals and gemstones could also work well to harmonize the land, but there's two issues with setting them outdoors. First is the exorbitant price that many homeowners are unable to afford, the other issue is theft. Anyone walking around could make off with them. Yet there are quartz-based stones that can be highly effective in transforming unhealthy meridians, namely large mica stone and Canadian Mountain Green. Both are veined with quartz. These rocks can be installed as single standing stones or in groups. A circle of large mica quartz stones I install totally transforms the murder energy rioting through a client's front yard and down the block.

In my first stone applications I'd come away surprised by how the rocks worked so well within the boundaries, topography and existing vegetation of a property. How precise and demanding the number, the configuration, and their placement. And ultimately, how effective they are in transforming the energy when the practitioner is attuned to their calling. It's as though there is a larger dynamic at work beyond my grasp and guidance. And the rocks and I are merely players in an intentional creation that brings another spirit, another architect to its formula and fulfillment.

With the outside treated and the most impactful meridians and areas transformed, the work then moves inside, free of that assault.

TIME FOR BED

The bed is a pivotal place in the health of the sleeper. For this reason, I check the energy radiating around it right away. These days I find myself in a lot of people's bedrooms! Even if the passing meridians have been treated and balanced, I may still recommend moving the bed. I'll explore the room for a healthier spot and finding one, encourage the people to move the bed there. A simple request you would think, but it can be a dramatic shift for many folks and on occasion I encounter firm resistance. The resistance can stem from a certain comfort level, or aesthetic sense. Some simply like the bed where it is. The size and shape of their bedroom may not lend itself to re-positioning the bed. Or, their Feng Shui perspective tells them the bed needs to face the door. In situations like this it's best to get creative, which may mean inviting them to explore the idea of sleeping in another place altogether and see if the symptoms dissipate and their health improves. The healing may take a while depending on their length of previous exposure.

BIOGEOMETRY INSTRUMENTS

As I mentioned previously, Dr. Karim has created a number of instruments that work to bring balance and beneficial energy to a space. When placed and calibrated appropriately, BioGeometry stands and dials can be effective in bringing a more harmonious energy to the interior of a home, clinic or office space. BioGeometry is an evolving science with new instruments being designed and refined for optimal harmonization.

There are many layers of treatments one can build on to create a healthier living space. The only instruments I'm hesitant to employ are those that require plugging into an electrical outlet.

FOLLOW-UP

'Check, re-check, and check again.' Such is the energy workers motto. One always needs to factor in potential changes that occur when a site integrates a shift in energy. Sometimes the treatments hold strong. Sometimes they need more work. Nothing is chiseled in stone – even when you're working with stone.

ENTITIES

Kathleen, a ghost buster friend, asks me to accompany her to a residence in St. Paul where she'd been asked to release an entity. Lost, traumatized and stubborn souls trapped or unwilling to exit the physical plane can leaden the energy of a space over time. One doesn't typically find a high vibratory level in areas where sinister ghosts reside. This particular resident ghost is fixed to a disturbed meridian. I watch as Kathleen stands in the middle of the meridian and opens her energy body to take in the space. From my point of view, it's like watching a big pink rose come into bloom. After about ten minutes, she steps away. The entity has been removed. Only the disturbed meridian remains, which I correct right outside with a large quartz-based stone. Disturbed meridians can attract disturbed entities. Density resonates to density. Some houses host a mardi gras parade of entities tromping through the rooms. Raising the vibratory rate of a place can shake off entities unable to exist in that energy field.

THE CLASSROOM

An elementary school teacher asks me to check out his 6th grade classroom. It is early September, a week before school is to start. The teacher is sensitive to the atmosphere of the room and the children's well being who must sit in one spot much of the day. He feels personally responsible for positioning any child's desk inadvertently in an irritated zone. Fortunately he has the liberty of setting desks wherever he wants, and not in straight, parallel rows. As it turns out, a number of his students would have experienced daily exposure to unheathy radiations.

Surveying another classroom in the same school, I discover a severely troubled spot in the room localized around one desk. "That's where a disturbed child sat for two years," the instructor shared. Which brings up the question: Was the spot imbalanced before the disturbed child came to the school and their personal imbalance resonated to that particular desk? Or was the spot affected by the energy emitted by the child who sat there for two years?

Leaving the school grounds I can't help but look back at all the desks in my years of public education that may have been situated on a zone of disturbance. There's just one big difference between my school years and now. Today's schools carry the additional background irritation of the electronic age.

PLAYFUL ENERGY

Not all energy treatments are 'by the book'. Sometimes a remedy bounces in out of the blue. Called on to survey a home in the Kenwood neighborhood of Minneapolis, I find a dark spot in the kitchen area near the primary energy center of the home. Setting river rock configurations and mica standing stones at precise places around the exterior transforms a number of incoming meridians. The energy on the main floor is balanced except for this one gnarly area of distress. I explore my bag of remedies - BioGeometry instruments, attachments, icons, only to come up short. So, I ramble through a litany of fringe treatments and find the space is calling for something belonging to the family, particularly Mary's young daughter, Hannah.

Mary jumps into the adventure, going about the house looking for photographs and other family-related items.

"I think I found it," I call out, baffled by the prospect of a white stuffed bear I spotted on the floor in a corner. Mary brings out a tall step stool for me to position the furry animal on top of the kitchen cabinet near the epicenter of the distressed energy.

"Funny," she remarks, "Hannah was going to give that away to a friend of hers just the other day but she changed her mind,"

"Uh-huh," I reply, stepping back down onto the kitchen floor, disbelieving the notion that a child's stuffed animal can bring about a positive shift in the field.

Yet, much to my surprise there is indeed a magical shift.

"Well, it's not exactly scientific, but it works!" I laugh, wondering why the space would call for something from the child of the house. Why would such a playful energy fill a void?

Mary brings out a historic ledger of the house that describes all the previous owners and occupants who had lived there. We find it interesting that the house had been occupied over the years by a series of single, childless men, and the last occupants who lived there had a very troubled child, who neighbor's claim was emotionally victimized by the father's alcoholism.

There are many modes to healing the energy of a site and with some exploration one may discover ways outside the normal channels.

SUPERIOR FORCES

In one suburban home, I find 'relationship battle energy.' I trace its center point to an area next to the bed in the upstairs master bedroom where it has become implanted there by the previous homeowners. Since the center of the emanation is right beside the bed, it does not lend itself to treatment with stones or BioGeometry devices. So, I decide to read, 'Call to Superior Forces' out loud on the spot of disturbance with the homeowner and see if it might help. I ask the homeowner to repeat the call seven times with me. Why seven times? Recurrence creates a current.

'Call of my heart. I call for those spiritual forces who are able to bring peace to this troubled site. I call for those Superior Forces who can help bring a healing touch from the source of caring to this place of distress. Let this touch release the hurt of times past. Let this touch allow this place to come to present time and be nourished in the belonging and harmony it now seeks. And from this day forward be transformed.'

As the homeowner and I repeat the call, I'm running my energy from the top of my heart down through my feet on down into the Earth. After only a couple incantations I hear a woman's voice quite clearly in the room say, "I'm sorry." After we repeat the prayer seven times, the agitated energy dissipates.

The French microvibrational scientists, Chaumery and deBelizal, attest to the efficacy of calling for help in neutralizing noxious waves, which they refer to as a psychic procedure. "This procedure is based on the call to the Superior Forces, a call always heard when executing it with perfect consciousness of one's own nothingness, and put in a state of love necessary to the success of such an operation. This makes it touch the failing Cosmic Forces and permits, by its intervention, the return to balance with the compensated forces."

ART FOR ENERGY'S SAKE

On a wintry, overcast day I'm surveying a lake cabin about fifty miles northwest of the Twin Cities. The client is a gifted painter who's become reluctant about continuing her art. Surveying her property I find an unhealthy line crossing diagonally through the front door into the cabin. As I point out the line to her, I notice a beautiful watercolor on the wall near the front entry - a muted landscape that depicts a tree-lined path with a corona of soft golden sunlight glowing among the boughs of trees giving the path an etheric quality that invites the observer into the scene.

"Is this one of yours?"

"Yes,' she says, "I painted it here."

On a lark, I unhook the painting from the wall and set it on the wooden floor by the front door, angling it directly in the path of the disturbed line. Then, checking the meridian, I find the energy has shifted and now the line is more balanced.

"Do you see what your art can do!" I exclaim. Her eyes swell, visually moved by the shift in the energy.

So, what is it about the watercolor that made the shift? Is it the intention of the artist? Is it the artist's caring for the subject matter, for nature, that went into the work? Is it the energy she was radiating when she painted it? Perhaps it's the pure enjoyment in the act of creating a beautiful picture? Or, all of the above. All I know is the watercolor transformed the agitation. Would it sustain the shift if left there? Perhaps not. But that's not the point. The point is that a work of art can help heal imbalances in the world in numerable ways, one being energetically. Truly, this is one of the extraordinary gifts artists and musicians bring to the world.

Artwork, artifacts and antiques may also broadcast toxic energy in a space.

WHAT WE BRING INTO OUR HOMES

While traveling in Southeast Asia, I purchased an unpainted mask on sight. Larger than a life, the mask expressed a menacing grimace with bulging eyes and ferocious fangs. It hung on the wall of my office facing my desk for years. One day I looked at it and realized the mask emits unhealthy energy into the room. And for good reason – warding off evil spirits and intruders was its intended purpose.

Sensitive to this, I keep an eye open when surveying homes and offices for the character of energy radiating from a piece of artwork, a sculpture, or a hand-me-down antique. It may be an item that has passed from generation to generation and along the way has become imprinted with an unsettling vibe. Or it may have been shaped to emanate a harsh energy field, and unwittingly, the owners hang it on the wall or make it the focal point of a room. One needs to be careful of heirlooms and antiquities. I've been in homes dramatically affected by relics and artwork that seethe with hostile energies, sometimes infecting more than one room.

COMMERCIALLY STAMPED VS TRUE TO SPIRIT

I answer the call to meet a client at a store where she wishes to purchase a couple mezuzahs, preferably ones that radiate a high vibratory level for her home. Mezuzahs are long, slender cases that carry within them Hebrew inscriptions of verses from the Shema prayer. Trained scribes pen the prayer on parchment with indelible ink. The parchment is rolled and set inside the case. The case is then affixed to the right side of a doorway from the point of view of the person entering.

Doorways are significant transitions in our lives, as mystics have long been aware. The doorway is a pivotal leverage point in which you can affect the energy and subsequent activity within the space by the quality of energy you emit as you pass the threshold. A blessing given in a doorway carries a stronger force than one pronounced in a room.

The store we visit carries drawer after drawer full of mezuzahs. I'm reading the energy of all types of mezuzahs in wood and silver and metal cases of various designs, symbols and colors. The energy of the verses is the important thing. Yet I'm surprised to find many mezuzahs radiating little or no energy at all, while others emit a high vibratory rate. What causes this difference? It isn't about the cost, because some of the more modestly priced mezuzah's in the store emanate as high and even higher vibratory rate than the more expensive ones. Since they're all located within inches of each other, the difference is not due to imprinting of the store energy. Is it that the prayer was penned on paper instead of sheepskin? I can only deduce that's it's about the level of life force instilled at the mezuzahs creation. As we well know, handmade items and clothing carry more vitality than manufactured or commercially stamped.

CLUTTER

"Please, excuse the mess." I hear this on countless occasions as I enter a home to survey the energy. All around are piles in corners, mail, magazines and newspapers heaped up on counters and under tables, boxes and accumulated odds and ends bulging from closets. Every horizontal surface over laden with unattended stuff. "I've been meaning to get to it. Haven't had the time."

These days, when my wife informs me that our house is a pit, I counter with, "This is nothing," which I state with resounding authority, having toured oodles of cluttered interiors. Not that it pacifies her. And she's right. If the pile sits there for days on end, a knot develops in the flow of energy in the space. Is the clutter affecting the energy or the effect of the energy of the place?

In a number of instances I find clutter sitting on a pre-existing area or intersection of disturbance. No wonder it lies there, gathering more clutter - our bodies are reluctant to venture into the broken or distorted energy field to clean it up because of the vibe. Who wants to feel that agitation?

So, in some situations it's not that we're lazy, or that we put off the headache of deciding to keep or toss every item that enters the home. Instead, our bodies are repelled by the energy of the spot and because of this we put off cleaning up the clutter. Talk about a marvelous excuse not to act! Still, the point is to keep the rooms clear.

Architect and author, Sarah Nettleton, shared with me an interesting insight. Summing up her many years in the home design business, she said, "Most clients come to me wanting to expand their homes when truly what they really need to do is cart away half the material possessions that overstuff their rooms and litter their lives."

CLOBBERED

Energy work is not something to go into lightly or blindly. It comes with ominous threats to one's health. These health hazards are given scant warnings in books and articles on the subject.

When dilating ones energy field to sense the existing energies or hone in on one particular target at a site, one must be mindful that the potential minefield they are stepping into may explode in their face. It's easy to become sick, or worse. Stories abound of people either oblivious, or feeling invincible, putting their lives in harm's way. Leon Chaumery, the French microvibrational scientist stands out as a tragic example of falling victim to noxious radiation.

Personally, I've been nailed on a number of occasions sticking my nose innocently or arrogantly into energies that are out to destroy anyone in their path. Imagine staring into the flared nostrils of a stampede of invisible, yet nonetheless real, rhinos.

The hostile energy may not be immediately obvious. It may be dormant until you come snooping along, digging into the energy of the place, stirring up the dust. Once the energy is named it becomes amplified. Too late – the monster has awoken. There are all manner of psychic shields, symbols, amulets, and things available touted to protect you from malevolent energies. What works for me is to be vigilantly mindful of the energy I'm in, nimble on my toes and ready to run. One particular incident comes to mind:

I'm treating a disturbed gridline in the backyard of a suburban property. I know the meridian is menacing, but I haven't ascertained the character and degree of imbalance. It feels broken. On my knees near the fence line I begin to feel nauseous. I set a BioGeometry stand on the ground to stabilize the incoming current as I work with water rocks to transform it. When I return home I feel poisoned. The energy has embedded itself in my body by hook and talon.

After a year in the field, I've come to believe we're all infected to some degree with the toxic energy we live in. So, how does one rid themselves of it?

CLEARING THE BODY

Geopathic Stress is known to accumulate in the body behind the neck in the brain stem region. Yet many toxic energies will go to a person's weak areas. These tend to be places in the body or energy body that resonate with them. These may be areas, organs, and chakras where you have been harmed and from where you do harm. One could say these forces highlight where a person is imbalanced, broken, damaged or dark.

There are a number of techniques for clearing your body after an encounter with toxic energies. I've come to rely on a lie-down mind's-eye body scan. This involves taking your time to make a thorough sweep of your body from under your feet up through the top of your head consciously searching for places of imbalance and concentrations of detrimental energy. The objective is to find the absolute core of the disturbance and release it. I always work with the pictures that are presented to me. If they are mechanical-looking, with gears and levers, then I'll dismantle them as a mechanic would unbolt an engine. If the image is reptilian in nature I will capture it in a net and remove it from my space. If I come upon a dark wad of knots, then I will disentangle them. The secret is not to judge or react to what you see or feel. It's simply an energy construct. Trap or unravel it and release it from your system.   This exercise can get thorny. Some energies can sink their hooks in you. They can masquerade as an aspect of your personality which makes it doubly tough to distinguish. I've spent up to an hour working to clear my body of harmful energies. So, it's important to allow yourself plenty of time to completely clear yourself. It is worth every minute. And the more you practice this visualization exercise the more sensitive you become to foreign energies entering your body and how to remove them.

If this visualization proves unsuccessful in clearing harmful energies, you may require assistance

in releasing them. Here it is best to seek one who is skilled in body clearing.

MAKING THE VIBRATORY SHIFT

In reassessing my year in the field treating properties, I discover what many in the healing profession already know. No matter how effective you are as a practitioner, if the patient (in this case the occupants of the home) cannot integrate the vibratory shift with their bodies, or if their behavior becomes unhealthy and they return to self-destructive patterns or emotions, such as cruelty, substance abuse and neglect, then the energy shift will suffer.

So the transformation needs to come about from both sides, the newly fortified emanations of the place and the inhabitant's effort to match and maintain the energy shift.

I've also become disturbingly aware how the people living at a disturbed site can carry a wallop. Afterall, they've been absorbing the energy for some time. This is important to know going in.

I'm called to check out a fairly new house in the western metro area. The homeowner has thrown up his hands with the place. Everything seems to have gone bad since he purchased the house – divorce, emotional turmoil, financial issues, etcetera. I find a number of disturbances, geopathic, historic and electromagnetic. After surveying the site remotely and physically I ask the homeowner to meet me ¼ mile away from the house at a more neutral site where I share my findings. Being so absorbed in the frenetic energy I feel the only way the homeowner will be able to clearly hear and understand my findings and recommendations is to be far away from the maelstrom of his home.

THE ENERGY GARDEN

Several years ago friends and I took part in transforming a barren, rock-hard vacant lot into a native tall grass prairie. The project took time to root and continues to be an education for us. Once the blue stem grasses, stiff golden rod, cone flowers and other native plants became established gathering bees and butterflies, I thought the new prairie had found its natural harmony and could be self-sustaining. Surely its diversity would serve to be its balancing scale. Little by little we expanded the prairie, and little by little we saw how certain plants began to dominate the field. So, the need to weed and limit became an annual custodial task.

The same holds true for energy work. You don't do it once and walk away. The energy garden needs constant, mindful attention to stay vibrant, life-giving and flower. Maybe 'need' is not the right word. The energy garden 'revels' in conscious touch. Revels in caring interaction, and it gives it back with bounty.

On several occasions clients have asked me, "Is it fixed?", or "Did you fix it?" A relevant question when it comes to the healthy energy of one's home and property. Unfortunately, this work is not like sealing a plumbing leak or replacing a broken window. Yes, detrimental energies are cleared away and a welcome balance is instilled. But, like gardening, this is not a do it once and it's a done deal. It's an ever unfolding adventure that requires ongoing conscious care and attention.

Things change. Energy is always on the move. Meridians are carrier waves, they are currents that can become contaminated by our activity, locally as well as from a distance. A housing development being built blocks away can affect the energy where

107

you live. Local hostilities, trauma, and pollution. There are also Earth changes to consider, axis and subterranean shifts, solar flares, cosmic winds, innumerable waves and particles circling and penetrating our lives. No dull moments here!

As in a garden, there are some extraordinary energies and dimensions inside and outside our lives. Some are medicinal, some help enliven the natural ecology and some are simply beautiful to behold. These energies need to be welcomed, honored, and given more breath. At the same time, there are also energies that work to dominate, distort and contaminate the more nurturing radiations. They can be highly invasive, pervasive and detrimental to the balance of the life of the place and in a broader sense, to the spiritual growth of the planet. These require vigilant, ongoing weeding out.

10

THE NEAREST GOD

"Hear the worms?" Larry murmurs, jutting a finger in the air. He's referring to the faint skitch of earthworms pulling leaves down from the forest floor. Larry Wade is a naturalist with a keen ear for calls and sounds. On many outings he's helped me open the spiral chambers of my ears to hear the far drumming of a pileated woodpecker, or distinguish the difference between the ratchety call of a kingfisher and that of a red squirrel. This time is no different. It is early spring. The air blushes with the rich smell of the land returning after a long winter freeze. The ground has come alive again with dirt movers chewing their fill and aerating the soil as night darkens the woods.

We continue along a path through the maple and oak trees - one of only a few remnants of the Big Woods, a vast forest that once covered 3,000 square miles of Minnesota before being logged in the 1800's. Further along the trail the percolating avalanche of peepers and cricket frogs draws us to the edge of a large wetland. Their incessant chorus throbbles the air. Talk about vibrations! It feels like it's aerating the cells of my body. Standing along the bank among the cattails, I wonder how these pulsations feed the forest. How the vibrations spread from the frogs overland through the Earth meridians. How far

109

it riffles out into space, perhaps resonating with some far off Frog Planet or Amphibia Constellation.

From what I've learned doing energy work, a diversity of sounds is symptomatic of a healthy site. A lack of natural sounds stunts growth. Natural sounds are more than auditory vibrations, they're also dimensions. A healthy energy field will have multiple dimensions created by the creatures inhabiting the site and those passing through - the flutter of butterfly wings, the deep hoots of a great horned owl, the scamper of a rabbit, a pond of trilling frogs. Add to this the seasonal waves of migratory birds broadcasting their calls across the high air overhead as they follow the magnetic Earth currents. Even the smallest no-see-ums participate in the sonic ecology of a place. All contribute to the aliveness of the land through invisible vibrations. They're like vitamins for the body. Trouble is, the world is losing natural sounds to the tune of more than 100 species a day. The very vibes that invigorate the energy body of the planet are going extinct like little breaths being snuffed out. A violin string vanishes. A note on the symphony sheet music blows away. Sounds that will not return or be reincarnated. And these are ones that are audible to our ears. How many sounds, essential to life, are we losing that are outside our range of perception? The no-hear-ums.

A number of times out walking with Donna Fortune, she'd say, "Listen to the tone of the Earth. Listen inside, with your inner ear and your heart together. Stop thinking. Simply listen. Listen without filters. What do you hear? Ask the land what it needs. The tone can tell you what is missing."

Or, when she would stop along a path and gently set her palm against the trunk of a tree and listen for its heartbeat the same way a doctor takes a patient's pulse. The heartbeat tells her the temperament of the tree's life force at that particular moment in time.

On one occasion, walking along a gravel road in New Grange, Ireland one afternoon she described the area as once having a great forest of huge trees that were chopped down and uprooted. Even the soil had been taken away. This happened long ago. The meridian was broken and four wise people killed by priests, their bones broken to kill their names. The land speaks to Donna and through her. "The tone of the land carries information past and present. The wind carries information of what's to come."

THE EARTH BODY

One of the ways Donna is able to hear the tone and sense the character of energies at a site is with what she calls the Earth Body. The Earth Body is a state of awareness that involves tuning ones body and soul to the body and soul of the planet. It is an amazing facility, yet for most people it sits dormant. Gaining access to one's Earth Body helps a person become more conscious and more understanding of the surrounding energy expressions of the natural world. The Earth Body is not something you create or a belief you acquire. Each one of us is born with this innate capability. It's pre-installed. Our physical bodies carry the water, the elements, the material composition and equations of the planet Earth. We are made of its clay and its gems. We are connected to the Earth in proximity, make-up and resonance. We are like mobile branches of the Earth tree and share an energetic bond, not unlike the blood bond between a child and its mother. And being in this resonance with the energy field of the planet there exists the capacity to be highly aware of the natural world in a true and intimate way.

For example, with her Earth Body, Donna is able to perceive the energy emanations of the land and its life forms in multiple dimensions and times. She can feel the communal aliveness of a forest interacting through the roots. She can hear the memories packed inside an age-old glacial boulder, touch the residual hurt of a riverbank from human neglect, see and hear the activities of devas and nature spirits, behold the brilliant colors of subterranean caverns and luminous crystalline clusters below her feet far beyond the visual reach of normal eyesight.

The Earth Body is not only a physical state of being, it also requires the etheric component, blending one's etheric soul with the soul of the Earth. This alliance of physical and etheric structures allows one to access new levels of knowledge. Knowledge that may simply spring into your mind one day with no memory or tangible source of where it came from.

Donna says, "When the Earth Body is alive, you immediately know what you need to do to keep the energy around you moving, to keep it all going. You know when there's danger in the air. You're also aware of your own impact. What will happen before you do something. If you do A, B, and C then D will happen. You know the consequences of your actions before you act."

Becoming mindful of the Earth Body I can't help but recall the elephants in Thailand who knew when the tsunami was coming and bolted for higher ground. Having a strong Earth Body allows information and communication to transfer more effortlessly between the planet and your body. So, strengthening your Earth Body will not only dramatically enhance your perceptual abilities, it may also save your life.

THE EARTH'S SOUL

When I chose to sense the planet's soul, it creates a shift in my field of perception. The simple admission brings new light to the air. Colors become more vivid. Natural surroundings are charged with an effervescent sparkle. The moment feels rich, more alive and my sense of participation in space is activated in ways I had not previously felt.

Telling others about the Earth's soul wrinkles eyebrows. It appears that many are tethered to a belief that souls are exclusive to human beings alone and since the Earth does not appear to have a brain like ours, think thoughts, dream dreams, or speak our language, it must be merely a resource for our nourishment and evolvement. A notion that has stuck with us since the dark ages and one I believe is keeping us there.

There are many ways to experience the Earth's soul. One way is to visit and connect in a caring and conscious way with a sacred site. These locations can be perceived as places where the Earth's soul surfaces to touch its completeness, which is a common experience for many who visit. A place that expands our sense of beingness, and being a welcome part of a greater, galactic, yet no less fragile life form.

As Donna has pointed out, "It is not necessarily sacred because it is good. It is sacred because it is a place where you feel whole."

When I feel my wholeness it's not an experience of ecstasy and levitation. I touch my strengths along with my weaknesses. I'm informed of my blockages and my flows. Areas that require attention are highlighted. A suppressed emotion or an issue I've been unwilling to share or accept comes into full view along with a more expansive worldview with boundless potential and possibility. Reality is no longer a projection of hard and fast rules and measurements. It is fresh air, fluid and infinitely free.

There are still places on the planet that radiate this quality of wholeness, this high vibratory spectrum of boundless energies in a complete and balanced way. Some of these are known and visited, while others are more remote, little known and less trafficked by people. Perhaps the planet sets some of these sites in hard to reach and less habitable places to safeguard the energy.

Sacred sites on the planet are not a place to build a home. As I informed the housing developers (Chapter 1), no one is entitled to build on such a site even if they purchased the title to the land. Being a source of wholeness, the site needs to be accessible to all. Wholeness is not carved to fit a certain doctrine or belief system, nor can it be owned, horded, or franchised. It is for all life forms to touch and to treasure, human and animal alike.

Throughout the centuries many religions have reflected this transcendental state of wholeness through the construction of magnificent temples and cathedrals. One steps inside grand gilded doors onto polished floors and is immediately uplifted by the towering ceilings and wondrous celestial domes. It is like entering a cavernous jewel illuminated by angelic shafts of sunlight pouring forth. No, this is not someone's home. This is God's house. The home of homes. The architectural embodiment of a holistic dwelling where the entire family of harmonic energies resides.

Although many a sacred site has been built upon, the land does not need churches, statues or cultural historic significance to be sacred. The Earth energy emanates wholeness all by itself.

Because of the higher vibratory rate that emanates from such a place, all kinds of unpleasant things can happen to people who build and live there uninvited. There's a higher incidence of alcoholism, drug use, divorce and corruption. And, at the same time, the vibrant energies that radiate from the site can become weakened and defiled by development and human habitation.

Why would anyone seek to destroy or defile a sacred site? Most folks have no intention of doing harm. Yet when we touch places unconsciously with our broken parts, the land takes in that brokenness and some of our personal energy remains stuck there as well. When we come to these places with our healthy parts, radiating conscious caring, it receives that and we walk away more enhanced by the experience.

There are also conscious forces that seek to break the land and disrupt harmony. They act openly and aggressively, as well as subtly, slyly undermining behind the scenes. These power levels definitely do not want anyone to experience, carry and radiate what is truly sacred and whole. They have clever ways of rationalizing their motives and hiding their actions. The result is what we see today in the extinction of species, the heating up of the seas, the depletion of oxygen, and a planet reeling in toxic energy.

The good news is more and more people are asking the question, "Why are we poisoning and defiling the very thing that gives us life?" The hard news is, the bigger the lesson, the bigger the crisis needed to learn it. So, it's looking more and more like it will take a global catastrophe of Biblical proportions to instill the importance of getting this planet off the ground and into our hearts.

Based on what I've learned in the field, our effect on the planet is not only physical, it is also energetic. This Earth absorbs and radiates the energy behind all our actions, emotions and thoughts. There is no ruler or measurement gauge when it comes to energy, so there's no difference between taking one small souvenir rock from Mt. Meru or one large one. The 'take' energy is felt the same - that of a trespassing leech. It's not about quantity or the relative value of the thing taken away, it's the quality or character of the energy within the action that the planet experiences, absorbs and reflects. All is seen, all is heard, all is felt, and these energies are then emitted from the scene of the incident and transported along the geomantic carrier waves and by the winds that cross the world.

Given my recent experiences in the energy fields, I surmise the all-seeing eye is the Earth's energy field. And, how we interact with our home planet, the nature of our caring and respect, the way we work to maintain and enhance its aliveness – this energy ripples out in waves. Just as rivers carry contamination to the oceans, the Earth meridians carry energy contamination to the etheric oceans. Our imbalance delivers imbalance outward into space. It is not just the physical life of the planet that requires immediate care, detoxifying and support, it is also its spiritual, vibratory life.

THE SPIRITUAL GROWTH OF THE EARTH

As I begin to see and accept the fact that this planet is a phenomenally creative, conscious living being with a soul, who has a purpose to fulfill, both physically and spiritually, a purpose all its own, outside of humanity's hopes and dreams, I begin to touch a deeper perception of things, a perception both magical and harrowing, and the question spills forth from my mind as from a cataract, "How am I helping to support the Earth's spiritual development?"

Sounds pretty highfalutin. Afterall, who knows the Will of the Earth? Who can say what kind of planet the Earth seeks to become? Yet, whatever this planet's spiritual quest may be, surely it is hobbled by the damage done to its energy fields.

When I imagine the Earth's body as if it is my own for a moment, it becomes achingly clear that such a conscious being cannot grow physically or spiritually when its energy meridians are so corrupted, and its life force bloodied and dimmed by human actions. Mother Earth must feel like a besieged parent, a sickened, unwilling servant to the brute species she feeds. Personally, I'd never doubted she would go on and on despite humanity's savage, insatiable appetite. Until now.

Sensing the consequences of our actions in surveying energy fields, I can no longer underestimate our capabilities. Now I wonder about geocide. I wonder if we've killed planets before and we're rutted in some nightmarish recurring pattern. To turn a well-known quote, we have met the energy and it is us. Yet, if people can impact a big planet in such a detrimental way, it is possible we can unite our energy fields with the Earth's energy field and work as one to re-enliven this world so that it radiates a high vibratory corona to the universe once again.

11

THE SPIRIT HOME

A year after Alex and Diane moved into their dream home things began to get interesting. The two-story corner house they designed together was one of the first to be built in a pastureland housing development. Quiet, close enough to schools and shopping, the location and the structure answered everything Alex and Diane desired, which they'd thoughtfully planned out to minute detail – an open, spacious kitchen attached to a family room, a wall of windows with southern exposure for passive solar gain, a roomy master bedroom with his and her closets, a huge lower level playroom for their two growing boys, and a grassy backyard sloping gently down to a duck pond.

Little by little, more and more houses popped up around them. 115 in all, powered by 220 volt electrical cable buried underground. As Alex and Diane began to enhance the landscaping around their home Alex became aware of an edgy, constricting feeling in his body whenever he walked around certain areas of his yard.

"I couldn't think clearly. My muscles would contract. Just being in the backyard gave me a headache. The longer I'd linger in the area the stronger the effect and the longer it would take to clear it from my body."

119

Sensitive to earth radiations and a practicing dowser, Alex discovered a wide meridian running diagonally within thirty feet of the house. The aggravated energy of the meridian also affected the balance of other meridians intersecting it and passing into the home.

Next door, the neighbor's redwood siding started to deteriorate before their eyes. Knowing how redwood is impervious to rot, Alex explored this oddity only to find the deterioration directly in the path of the agitated energy line. In the next house over, the meridian clipped a boy's corner bedroom. A boy who had been suffering serious respiratory illnesses, asthma, and allergies, since the family moved in.

For Alex, it became clear that the increase in electromagnetic radiation created from miles of newly buried electrical cable coursing through the ground of the housing complex had upset the natural energy flow of the Earth meridians. Living in the house for only a year, Alex no longer wanted to be there anymore, while Diane could not consider the idea of leaving.

Alex and Diane's dream house had turned into a nagging problem to solve. So, Alex sought to balance the line by applying a number of energy treatments. He began by placing water rocks at different spots along the disturbed meridian.

"It was like flipping a switch. The positive change was that sudden."

He color-balanced the entire backyard, driving ten wooden stakes, each painted a different color, at specific dowsed spots around the perimeter. He then went about the interior of the house color balancing the rooms with small dots of color placed at prime places on the walls.

"Still, I felt that in time, due to the severity of the energy and the impending home building boom there, the treatments would not hold."

After two years and admirable efforts to bring balance to their home, Alex and Diane decided to move. Their next door neighbors moved as well.

Could there be thousands of people like Alex and Diane whose dream house is turning into a nightmare? Yes, with one significant difference - Alex and Diane are aware of disturbed Earth energies. Other folks don't know why things are falling apart.

LOCATION, LOCATION, LOCATION

Builders and architects are familiar with many invisible hazards to human health, such as radon (the gaseous breakdown of subterranean uranium-rich materials), carbon monoxide from the back-drafting of furnaces and water heaters, as well as airborne spores from mold and mildew. There are plenty of inspectors and specialists for these, but nary a one for examining the health impact of the energy mush created by the combination of contaminated Earth meridians, electromagnetic fields, and underground radiations from fissures and streams. Nor are there any land developers with geomancers on staff to assess the energy radiating from the construction site to see if it's conducive to building healthy homes.

Realtors chant, "Location, location, location." And it's true – just not in the way they mean it. After surveying million dollar homes chockfull of noxious energy one realizes that it doesn't matter if the house is 10,000 square feet and the architect is Frank Lloyd Wright. It doesn't matter if the house is 'built green' and the ground breaking ceremony took place during a fruitful moon. What truly matters is the energy that emanates from the site.

A person dwelling in a cave may experience more healthy and enlivening energy than a person who resides in a luxurious mansion. Certainly the shape and features of a house can have an influence on the energy inside. The caring and harmony of the occupants will also promote a nurturing energy field.

121

Yet the underpinnings for one's quality of life are fundamentally tied to the spirit of place. And this awareness is outside the reality of today's home builders and consumers.

Buying a new home is the largest financial investment most folks make in their lives. If it's a brand spanking new home the buyer automatically expects it to be a healthy, safe, durable, and comfortable place to live. It's new, how can it not be? Consumers today are more informed than ever. Yet how many folks consider the home's placement on the property, the prevailing earth radiations and the vitality of the nature spirits? How many are aware of the pollution and trauma endemic to the manufacture of the home's materials? Or the energy embedded in the home by the attitudes of the architects, builders, trades people and designers who worked on it?

Truly there is a lot to consider. And it's not as though builders don't already have enough on their plate.

THE WHOLE HOUSE

Mark LaLiberte is a passionate home building specialist who flies around the country teaching residential architects and contractors the physics involved in what he calls 'the whole house systems approach" to new home construction. This approach is firmly tied to building science and looks at the entire house as an organism of interconnected parts working as one. Although the materials may differ, from the exterior siding and windows, to the interior woodwork and the mechanicals, all the elements need to work together to make the home safe, sound, breathable, energy efficient, affordable to buy and maintain, and resource efficient with minimal impact on the environment.

A home built with the whole house systems approach is constructed well beyond the guidelines of the Universal Building Code. Many homebuyers believe that a new home built to code is of high quality. But code is a minimum set of performance standards. It's the lowest common denominator a contractor can legally build. And Mark has seen many a new code-built home fall apart with the contractor subsequently facing litigation.

One day walking a construction site, Mark shared with me how far the quality of home craftsmanship has deteriorated over the years. This decline is partly due to the lack of cohesion and continuity between crews in different stages of the building process. A typical new American home is built by a series of trades people - foundation installers, rough carpenters, electricians, plumbers, heating and ventilation installers, roofers, masons, drywall installers, finish carpenters, to name a few. All these individuals and teams overlap each other during the stages of construction, sometimes stepping on each other's work.

Making the home building process one seamless, team-connected flow is a challenge, and typically there's little contiguous oversight and inter-communication during the planning and construction. So, not only is the energy of the site disregarded, the vision of the house being a united body of integrated systems is overlooked as well. What you have is a patchwork quilt instead of an interwoven rug. As Mark has seen while inspecting new homes in nearly every state of the country, there is a horrific number of hurried and botched installations hidden within the walls with disasters waiting to happen.

A phone call from Jim, a home building acquaintance, sheds more light on today's residential construction practices. After sending me a plan to survey for his new home outside Lancaster, Pennsylvania he tells me how over the years he's become less impressed and more frustrated with the workmanship and the attitude of contractors and construction crews in his region of the country. He's decided to hire Amish to build his new home because, "They're quiet, organized, and they honor the spirit and the craft of home building."

Although Jim may not be someone open to the reality of invisible energies, his observation is a testimonial to their relevance. There's more to quality home construction than the tightness of the fit and finish. The unseen energy of the work that goes into the construction is also of lasting value.

Recently, while surveying a remodeled suburban home, I picked up anger energy radiating from the cinderblock foundation of the new addition. Turns out the source of the anger came from the remodeling contractor! Whatever upset he felt at the time of setting the block, or friction between him and the homeowner, this emotional energy became lodged in the outside bedroom wall of the homeowner's young daughter. Since the remodel, the girl had felt ill at ease in her new bedroom. She couldn't articulate the reason, only that she didn't like being in the space and preferred to sleep in another room. What does this tell us about our creations and the impact our emotions and thought forms have on the work we do?

From the gathering and manufacturing of the building materials to the mode of energy employed in its construction, new homes radiate very little caring, if any at all. Most are sterile at best. They are an object. A product. One could say that the whole 'caring thing' is expected to kick in with the new homeowners, not the home builders. You can't expect the carpenters, electricians, plumbers and roofers to pour love into walls, now can you?

Several years ago I pitched an idea for a television series to the Home and Garden Channel called, "The Enlightened Home. I'd created and produced other series for them and thought they might be ready for something earthy, innovative, and ultra green.

"Enlightened? What's that? Sounds spiritual. Could mean anything. No, that's not for our audience," was the reply. They didn't even give me the nominal minute and a half to elaborate. Not that I could. I didn't really know what the overall scope of the show would be, but like so many things, I knew it would present itself once I jumped in. So I wrote it up anyway and stuffed it in a drawer for another day.

I did know the TV series would document the siting, design and building of an all-natural house that respected the nature spirits, natural life forms and topography of the land. A home constructed with caring and craft, oriented for the seasons, the arc of the sun, the moon and the constellations. We'd bring all flavors of experts on the show, from Feng Shui masters, to innovative off-the-grid wind and solar power experts, landscapers and rain and snow specialists who design gardens and roofs to optimize rain fall. We'd also feature some fearless American architects like Kendrick Bangs Kellogg, and Bart Prince to present a number of wildly inventive home design options.

Pitching the show today, I'd push to make it even more 'enlightened', steering the concept toward an even more holistic and energy conscious home. The following ideas are things I'd want covered over the run of the series based on what I've learned from my time working in the energy field.

BUILDING AN ENERGY-CONSCIOUS HOME

Safety comes first. We would consider the stability of the area. It boggles the mind the places people build their homes, on eroding ocean cliffs, in hurricane zones, on the foothills of volcanoes, atop known fault lines, in flood plains, as well as desert areas that require miles and miles of channels

125

engineered to pump water from faraway lakes and dammed up rivers.

We would look for land that emanates a high degree of aliveness and multi-dimensionality. This is manifested visually by the diversity of animals and vegetation as well as the vitality of the nature spirits and other dimensional beings who inhabit the area.

As the Bhutanese monks humbly entreat the deities of the land for agreement to build, we would also honor the existing guardian spirit of the place and seek its permission and counsel. Afterall, we are stepping into someone else's home. If you were the land and someone came looking to build a house on you, certainly you'd want them to respect and enhance your aliveness or stay out.

We would value the existing topography, natural formations and the rocks and trees. We would devote as much land as possible to the wild by creating a wide greenway or corridor of native wilderness between yards. These wild areas would not be managed or mowed or trod upon, but set aside for nature to be nature and for nature spirits to have a place all to themselves, free of the human factor.

We would honor the rocks. North America is roiling in angry rocks that have been bulldozed, dumped, crushed, dredged up from their homes, and utterly disregarded as conscious beings. It's one thing to be rolled about by a glacier or submerged by an ocean, and quite another to be heartlessly knocked around by the bidding of unconscious humans manning tractors and forklifts.

We would honor the trees. Flying over towns and neighborhoods I not only see the lack of trees in proportion to the asphalt and the buildings, I feel the imbalance in my bones. Every household plot of land needs more trees especially deciduous trees like maples and ginkos - trees that generate much needed oxygen for the Earth's atmosphere.

Before designing the new home, a thorough energy survey of the grounds would be conducted. We would look to see if there are any underground streams, blind springs, fissures, unhealthy mineral deposits and areas of contamination or anti-life energies. We would note the beneficial aspects as well, those areas that radiate high vibratory energies. We would look for ways to integrate these areas into the overall design so that they can be amplified.

We would design and orient the home in accordance with the cardinal compass points. We would set the walls in precise alignment with the natural meridians of the planet. Recent discoveries have found that these energy meridians were used in the design and placement of ancient monuments, pyramids, temples and palaces. In many cases the walls were placed directly along the grid lines and the columns or centers on grid crossings. Why would ancient builders construct the walls on the geomantic meridians? Seemingly so that the structure would grow naturally out of the radiant energy currents of Earth. Building this way strengthens the wall's durability and increases the longevity of the structure. All the better to last the test of time.

Visiting Cambodia and the temple complexes around Angkor Wat one realizes how keenly aware the temple architects were of Earth radiations. They studied the natural grid lines of the Earth, designing and constructing their elaborate stone buildings to integrate these energies. In one instance I find the distance between grid lines tightly compressed outside the walls of a structure. As I approach the steep steps of the building I run into a series of grid lines right outside in very close proximity to each other - while inside the building there are none to be found.

In her book, *Points of Cosmic Energy*, Blanche Merz delves into this phenomena of moving or compressing grid lines in close proximity to each other outside a building, which she herself explored at an Egyptian temple. How'd they do it? No one knows. Why did they do it? The author suggests that in distant times, people didn't move at today's pace of life. And crossing these gridlines before entering a temple, "...invited them to halt, meditate and prepare for crossing the next threshold."

Having the gridlines outside would also minimize the affects of irritated incoming energy streams on the interior of the structure. I also wonder, since meridians are communication lines, if by moving them outside the temple, the activities inside would be free of interlopers, free of telepathy. Psychic spies or sorcerers would not be able to tap into the meridian and eavesdrop on what is happening or being spoken within the walls of the temple.

How the ancients were able to move these Earth meridians is another question.

Following the example set by the Feng Shui masters of old, we would honor the timing of the construction. Just as there are beneficial times for planting seasonal crops and trees, there also auspicious times to break ground and plant a house. We would organize the construction of the home in accordance with favorable positions of the stars as they align with the timing and star charts of the new occupants.

For our homes and communities to be of lasting durability today's architects and builders can take a lesson from the ancients - design structures in concert with the physics and metaphysics of the site and not in ignorance or defiance of them. Creative expression is a marvelous freedom. Creative expression that impedes or distorts the life force of the land is an indulgence the world can little afford.

Best to select an architect who is aware of Earth energies and who ascribes to designing homes that work in accord with the natural currents of the planet. Someone like Dr. Ibrahim Karim, or an architect schooled in his BioGeometry science and who employs the energy of shapes, the quality of center, sacred ratios and numerical values - design applications that stimulate a harmonic vibration throughout the structure.

We would look at the context in which the building materials and resources are gathered and manufactured, avoiding those that tax our natural resources and that carry traumatic or self-interest energy such as clear cut old growth redwood and cedar lumber. The pain of their mechanized slaughter radiates from the shingles and decks they become.

The jury is still out on powering the home. Electricity is tricky. I may be alone in this but I believe when it comes to technology, less is more. The less technology, the more freedom I have, and the less dependent I am on a highly complicated yet fragile system which at any time can shut down leaving me in the cold and in the dark. Not to mention the harmful electromagnetic frequencies these household conveniences emit.

Where this matters the most is the bedroom where studies show how electromagnetic fields (EMF's) may upset sleeping patterns through the disruption of the pineal gland's secretion of melatonin, the body's sleep inducer. How can you wind down, de-stress and drift asleep easily when the background buzz of electricity has your pineal gland on alert.

Better to make the bedroom an EMF-free zone - free of TV sets, cellular phones, telephones, and electric alarm clocks. A couple bedside table lamps, a general ceiling light and a battery operated alarm clock would suffice. I would minimize the roping of electrical wire in the walls of the bedroom, and install a remote system that at the touch of a button will shut off all the juice to the room. Make sleeping as restful as camping out under the Milky Way.

When it comes to applying chemicals, we'd apply heavy restrictions. Pesticides, herbicides, fungicides, all the 'cides' (which means, 'to kill') can have a destructive effect on the life force of the land. Surveying a number of properties I've found that these manmade poisons deplete the soil of its innate growing abilities. They take the tools out of the hands of nature's workers and eliminate nature spirits. These poisons can stay in the soil for years and years. It basically becomes inert dirt or as Donna Fortune once noted, "The life force is dead. It's like walking on nothing." And, ultimately these poisons work their way into the groundwater. What goes on the land, goes into the water.

Instead of applying 'cides,' we would seek to balance the land and insect population with energy treatments and feed the soil with living humus from an organic compost pile.

CURVE THE WATER

Watching my wife water the garden from a hose one day I came to wonder if the straightness of the conveyance dulls the vitality of the water. Water in nature does not flow in a straight line. It meanders and forks its way from snowy mountain melt trickles and watersheds to streams and rivers. It becomes churned by rocks, ribbed and eddied by swift moving currents and jettisoned into foam from cascading heights. The flow of drinking water through our bodies also bends and branches through the inner BioGeometry of the human anatomy. There are no straight paths as such but multiple spirals and switchbacks as the water descends this inner mountain. Yet the water in our homes runs up walls and under floors through copper and plastic pipe in rifle-barrel direct lines.

How does this straight arrow motion affect the energetic quality of the water? How does it affect our bodies and the trees and plants we water?

Curious, I checked the energy of my well water running through a straight garden hose. The water gave off a flat vibration with low vitality. So, I called my plumber to see if he'd be willing to create an alternative hose for an experiment. I drew up a sketch showing a length of copper tubing with sixteen consecutive clockwise spirals and an adaptor soldered to the end to attach to my garden hose. He came back with the exact replica of my plan along with the addition of a shut off valve. I ran well water through the new apparatus and found the energy quality to be significantly enhanced. I then set up a little test with two raised beds of tomato seeds using the same planting soil in each bed and the same tomato seeds. The tomatoes watered from the spiral hose grew fuller than those watered with the straight line hose and plant for plant the spirally watered tomatoes emitted enhanced vibrations. The contour of the path shapes the energy. Surely more research and testing needs to be applied to the notion of a spiral water distribution system before jumping to any quasi-wondrous conclusions. This test used a simple recurring spiral. There may be further energetic enrichment of the water with tighter spirals or other geometric configurations.

HIRING HOME BUILDERS

The energy of the workers is left behind after their work is done. It permeates the land, the structure and the construction materials. How do you inform a builder and the subcontractors that their attitude plays an influence in the quality of energy they put into the home they build? How do you require them to only run 'good' energy. You really can't. It needs to be deep in their nature and enjoyment of their craft. But, you can be attentive to who you employ. We would hire builders and subcontractors based on their affinity for their work. We would visit a site where they are building a home and observe first hand the energy they emit as a team. We'd also help set up the energy of the site so that it was organized, safe, and schedule the work with timely yet pressure-free goals.

Interviewing former President, Jimmy Carter during an intensive Habitat for Humanity project on a reservation in South Dakota, I learned the intrinsic value of home ownership. President Carter spoke about the difference between renting and owning one's home. How people take more responsibility when the home belongs to them than if they're simply renting it or leasing it. This can show in the upkeep and the energy given. Ownership creates a bonding attachment that renting or leasing does not fulfill.

From my experiences surveying the energy of properties, I've come to look at the 'home' in a new way. I've come to see that it is not simply a sheltering need, it is a fixed place of ongoing interaction between the etheric and physical worlds. Whether it's a big house, a small house, or an apartment is not important. Wherever I live, there is an Earth meridian near me - a moving stream that conveys and exchanges energy to the entire geomantic circuitry of the planet. So, the quality of energy I instill and nurture in the place where I live not only affects the structure, the yard and the neighborhood, it also has repercussions worldwide.

To create an enlightened, or 'spirit home' is to understand one's physical and etheric responsibility, and to live in accordance and agreement with the spirit of the land. A 'spirit home' enhances the aliveness of the inhabitants and the Earth. In this creative alliance the occupants and the Earth energies donate to each other's existence in physical harmony and spiritual growth. This home is not a 3 bdrm, 2 bath, maintenance-free 'thing'. It's an ever-changing life-form that gives and receives on multiple energy levels. The shell may not change shape, but the space and the occupants are always becoming.

12

MEETINGS WITH REMARKABLE ENERGIES

Jim Kreider is a psychotherapist who teaches at the University of Kansas. He conducts his therapy work out of his home on a lazy tree-lined street in Lawrence. His upstairs office includes a large group therapy space and a smaller, more intimate room devoted to individuals.

Jim is standing in the doorway as I slowly circle his office assessing the energy. He knows me well enough to accept my theatrical nature as I blurt out my impressions of the space with each step, "Uh-oh," I gulp by the chair. "Whoa," I moan, standing over the couch. "Your clients sit here?" And, moving to his desk, my skin contracts, "Ooo!," I yowl.

All around the perimeter of the room the energy is battered and unhealthy. I pivot and take two steps to the center of the room where I feel a sudden, tectonic shift. My shoulders gently drop. Breathing returns. "Ahhh." It's like stepping into a slender fountain of clear, effervescent energy the girth of my body.

Puzzled by the dramatic change within a three foot distance, I make another orbit of the room – stepping over to his desk, "Ooo..." Then, two steps to the center, "Ahh." Jim's face appears perplexed as he watches me teeter-totter, ooing and ahhing back and forth between the chairs and couches and the center of the room... "Ahhh."

Finally I turn to him and sum it up, "The space is hurtin' everywhere except for this spot where I'm standing. This is good."

"You mean my clients sit in a harmful energy?" he asks.

"Afraid so. It's rough and ragged everywhere except right here in the middle of the room. The energy here is great. Why that is I can't say just yet. It just is."

"That's where I clear myself each morning before I see people," Jim says.

"Really. Care to show me."

I step out of the way as Jim pulls the chair from his desk and rolls it to the center spot. He sits down, takes a deep breath and explains his morning routine, "I sit here for about 15 minutes working to ground my energy deep into the earth, open my heart and free my body of judgmental thoughts and negative emotions so I can be there for the people who come to me for help."

"Everyday?" I ask, orbiting him, checking the energy field.

"Every morning I'll be seeing people."

Although the field of healthy energy only extends the circumference of Jim's chair, it's clear to me that his morning ritual has an effect on what otherwise would be a completely unhealthy space. A welcome oasis in a combat zone.

With some outdoor stone energyscaping to calm the jagged incoming currents, Jim's entire office is balanced. Now when he clears his body and mind, the heartfelt energy he works to radiate blooms beyond his chair and fills the room.

Jim's clearing exercise is a good example of how our bodies are emitters capable of transforming the energy of the space we inhabit, however small.

The human body's energy field – the radiant corona surrounding the body – is a vibrational muscle that carries surprising capacity and scope. And like a muscle, with exercise it can grow and become a vital force in transforming the space around it.

Here's a simple exercise. Recall a memory of a great moment in your life and rerun it in your heart and mind. Select a memory when you felt really good about yourself and the world. A moment in time when you felt whole, free and alive. Picture it as vividly and deeply as you can. Once you feel it, allow the sensation to flow out from every pore of your body. Keep breathing as you work to sustain the current. All your attention is on releasing this quality of the energy into the space around you. Keep breathing. Now, inflate your energy field a little further. If you set aside a place to practice this exercise everyday, you may find that the place retains the energy and becomes a source of aliveness for you every time you sit there.

I believe that as a person intentionally exercises and stretches their body's energy field over time their sixth sense will become heightened. They will become more attentive to the invisible energies surrounding them - energies that are favorable to the wholeness of life and the balancing force of Nature, and those that block or undermine it.

THE EVERLIFE & THE ANTI-LIFE

The more I survey the energy of places, the more energy appears to me in three primary faces. Two of these energies are in tune with and favorable to life. These two are always on the move in a continuous flow. The first toward growth or gain. The second toward re-shaping and re-transformation. Together these two energies unite in a ceaseless continuum or Everlife, for need of a word.

The compost heap is a good example of the Everlife. The skin of an avocado, a carrot top, the husk of a corn cob, once fully formed vegetables and fruit are given a special place to decompose and rematerialize into nutrient soil that creates a foundation for the growth of new vegetable matter. Energy forms re-forming to feed new energy forms. Although the discarded vegetable matter may be dead by our definition, it is still surfing the greater energy wave. In the Everlife, death is not an end where energy is concerned. Natural death is an eternal bed of becoming. (*)

The third face of energy is a non-flow state. It is not a natural living or natural dying movement. It is in a blocked or non-becoming state. Neither growing to flower and fruit nor decomposing into nutrient humus.

This Anti-life state undermines the Everlife. It drains the Life Force. It is more than simply an imbalance – it is a paralyzer. If we could release this anti-life from our lives, from our minds and our actions, it would go a long way to revitalizing the world. As my friend, Dr. Harlan Mittag aptly pointed out to a group attending one of our workshops, "We don't know what good really is."

Some would call anti-life energy evil. My understanding of evil is the enjoyment in doing repeated acts of harm without remorse. The word, 'evil' is charged with religious fervor. It brings to mind demonic and horrific acts of violence. Anti-life energy is definitely that. It is also inconspicuous and elusive. It suppresses aliveness in slow drips as it promises comfort and easy gratification. Whether we call it evil, anti-life, or just plain bad doesn't really matter as long as we recognize its dense, rigid, flat energy that seeks to remove identity, silence voice and song and shrink everything down to one dimension.

Seeing anti-life energy in the outside world is one thing. Seeing where I harbor it within myself is eye-popping to say the least! I continue to exhibit anti-life energies in the form of broken-record behavioral patterns, impatient knee-jerk reactions and emotional masks. The demons show themselves in my interactions, belittling self-talk, wanting things my way, and unwillingness to accept life as it is. These imprints are in continual resonance with matching energies in the outside world that trigger them again and again.

I'm also finding that running Life Force energy requires a highly attentive effort. You don't simply flick a perpetual motion switch and go about your business. There is no auto-pilot for this kind of energy consciousness work - I've looked! To sustain my awareness of center with caring and compassion in the midst of passing thoughts, stirred emotions and a world of pending change requires vigilant guided attention - attention to my grounding, attention to my heart, and attention to my field of attention.

I'm beginning to believe that effort is everything when it comes to overcoming anti-life energy. Where comfort, control and indifference can be seductive, efforting moves energy, creates new waves, new patterns and a higher vibratory level that makes it tougher for the denser, anti-life energies to attach.

If you've ever stood beside an ancient bristlecone pine, or seen a tree growing up through a crack in solid granite, with only a modicum of soil and moisture, you've seen the everlife energy in vivid slow-motion action.

According to Donna Fortune, "Every struggle we say 'no' to, we say yes to becoming less than we are." On the other hand, by seeking growth and transformation, solving problems, overcoming obstacles and stretching one's consciousness we help erode the anti-life energies inside and outside us.

THE BODY'S GREATER BODY

Dr. Manning has tears in her eyes as she hikes up the hill toward the gathering group of us. "I'm okay," she says, wiping her eyes, "I don't fear the Earth anymore." She just participated in one of the exercises in an Earth Energy workshop. The outdoor workshop is designed to help people become more grounded, centered and open energy bodies to better experience and connect with the Earth's energy body. This particular exercise I call, "Walking Inside Your Greater Body." The exercise serves as an outside-is-inside mobius shift in perception. Instead of viewing reality as 'me-here and everything else out-there', one begins to look at the world from the point of view that 'everything outside is inside.' You are walking inside your body's body. (*)

The first time I experimented with this shift of perception I became excessively sensitive to everything around me. Man-made technologies became foreign invaders in my system. I wanted to topple power lines and put an end to all motorized vehicles. I felt assailed by the cacophonous drone of fuming machinery in my greater body and I wished them banished immediately. A bit extreme you might say. Another time walking in my body's body I saw how features of the natural world are in fact our external organs. The forests, our outer lungs; the rivers, our outer circulatory system. I saw how spirit and water are intimately woven together and as we contaminate rivers the vitality of our spiritual lives becomes weak, rigid and defiled. For a while after that I became obnoxiously ecovangelistic! So, if you ever practice this outside-is-inside perception, be careful, you may not be able to stomach some of the more caustic worldly things currently happening inside your body's greater body.

OUTSIDE-IS-INSIDE CONSCIOUSNESS

The familiar axiom, "As above, so below," attributed to Hermes Trismegistus is a wonderful perspective that illustrates the resonant tissue between the physical and spiritual energy fields and the influence each has on the other. What occurs in the physical plane has repercussions in the etheric. What occurs in the etheric plane affects the physical.

Expanding on Hermes, I've come to see how outside and inside also work hand in hand. As outside, so inside. The inner and outer worlds share aspects, attributes and influence of the same life force. What happens in the outside world affects and reflects our inside world and the other way around. A dammed-up river outside is a dammed-up energy current inside.

This shift in world view opens the aperture of perception wide. The great outdoors becomes immediately intimate. A wondrous and immense intimacy that presses one to feel a more energetic responsibility. If the outside world is inside me then, yikes! How am I honoring it? How am I fortifying it? How am I poisoning it? Neglecting it? Replenishing it? The more mindful I am of this outside-is-inside perception, the clearer I am about what needs to be done in my own backyard.

Many health-minded people are extremely careful about what they put into their bodies in the form of organic food and nutritional drink. What am I putting into my body's greater body? What items and materials am I purchasing whose design and manufacture generates or discharges anti-life energy? If any aspect of it does not nurture the greater body, how can it possibly nurture me?

This Outside-is-Inside point of view also creates a dimensional shift. A shift that has helped me understand the difference between random inventiveness - manifesting a multitude of things with little if any consideration of the consequences and more mindful Greater Body inventiveness. Creating from a Greater Body mindset, one would more consciously and completely consider the well spring of the idea, the path it travels, the end of its stream and the ramifications in between. In other words – how does it enhance the garden? Case in point – nuclear power plants. Burying nuclear waste in the Earth would not be acceptable in a Greater Body dimensional creation. You're simply stuffing it deeper inside your body's body! Anything emitting harmful EMF radiation would go back to the drawing board. The health impact of every invention and product would be thought through with caring precision. More heart, more long-haul speculation and lots of cud chewing in the Greater Body dimensional state! By asking, 'does the creation nurture the vitality of the Earth and other life forms?' we may find that many of our manifestations would not make the cut. And those that proceed to fruition would resonate to a wider vibratory spectrum of life.

Obviously to reach such a state of energy-mindful manifestation is a pipe dream. We would need a seismic, cross-cultural sea change, or a massive crisis of Noah's Ark proportions to set it in motion. Still, a thousand energy-conscious miles begins with one energy-conscious step.

A YEAR IN THE FIELD

After a year in the field I've become much more energy-conscious of the world I inhabit. I've come face to face with a multitude of toxic energies I'd not been previously aware. These natural and manmade energies may appear to be innocuous, but actually, they impose an undermining influence on our immediate and future lives because they attract and incite more of the same harmful energies.

I've also met remarkable energies capable of inducing magical and transformative healing and change. And I've learned how we are potentially phenomenal emitters ourselves. Our energy body is capable of stretching far beyond the flesh and intentionally blending with healthy Earth energies deep in the ground to help clear distortions and past trauma from a site. Although this is far easier to say than to do, I believe this is the work ahead of us. The work of clearing the Earth of detrimental energies so a healthier, more radiant field of energy may thrive. It's a new dimension of stewardship. The dimension of energy gardening. There is no boundary between our bodies and the greater body of the Earth. Outside is inside. By healing injured lands we begin to heal ourselves. Like planet, like body.

I believe that as we travel along the path of energy gardening we will discover an ever greater spectrum of conscious and nourishing energies at hand. Some, I surmise, have tucked themselves in the depths of the Earth safely awaiting the ravenous hurricane of humanity to pass. Further along the path I believe we will meet more remarkable energies residing in uncharted nooks and dimensions that only show themselves to those who can resonate to their higher vibratory field. And, once we resonate to them, they were there all along.

I invite the curious and the naysayers to take the leap and spend a year in the field. To explore the world of energies we live in with open-minded scrutiny and see what the invisible reveals. If my experience is an indicator, you will discover buried treasure you've been side-stepping all these years.

NOTES

Chapter 3

DIVINING
I use the terms dowsing and divining interchangeably. Whether one is energy dowsing, locating underground water or crystal-balling future events, to me dowsing and divining both signify a search. A search for the truth.

Chapter 4

SUPERFUND SITES
Currently there are more than 1,000 Superfund Sites in the US.

Chapter 6

PERMISSION TO DOWSE
There are three questions commonly asked by dowsers around the country prior to conducting a search or survey:

MAY I? Do I have the permission of the person or subject I am about to dowse?

CAN I? Am I physically and mentally able to dowse accurately at this time? Do I have the necessary skills?

SHOULD I? Is now an appropriate time and place to dowse for the good of all concerned?

By asking permission a dowser is acknowledging that he or she may not know all the ramifications connected with the dowsing they're about to perform. The very act may be a stressor, an untimely intrusion into something or someone beyond their awareness at the time. So, it's always best ask first. Respect the spirit of the place, the person or the object of attention before going ahead.

Chapter 7

GOLD ENERGY

In his books, "Unveilied Mysteries, and The Magic Presence, Godfre Ray King speaks of this level of gold energy.

"Gold is placed upon this planet for a variety of uses, two of its most trivial and unimportant ones being that of using gold as a means of exchange and for ornamentation. The far greater activity and purpose of it, within and upon the earth is the release of its inherent quality and energy to purify, vitalize and balance the atomic structure of the world."

"Gold is one of the most important ways by which energy of the sun is supplied to the interior of the earth, and a balance of activities maintained. As a conveyor of this energy, it acts as a transformer to pass the sun's force into the physical substance of our world, as well as to the life evolving upon it. The energy within gold is really the radiant, electronic force from the sun, acting in a lower octave. Gold is sometimes called a 'precipitated sun-ray.'

"As the energy within gold is an extremely high vibratory rate, it can only act upon finer and more subtle expressions of life, through absorption."

"In all "Golden Ages,' the metallic form of gold was in common use by the mass of mankind; and during these periods, its spiritual development reached a very high point of attainment.

One reason for the chaos of the present time, is because the Gold in the commercial world is being hoarded, instead of being allowed to flow freely among mankind; and carry its balancing, purifying energizing activity into the commercial life of the race.

The hording of gold in great quantities means an accumulation of Inner force which if not released within a certain time will release itself by the overcharge of its own Tremendous Inner power."

Chapter 8

ABOUT PHYSICAL TRANCE MEDIUMS:

"The oracles, the physical trance mediums have always been typically the people that the Earth has worked through for humans. A physical trance medium's purpose is to actually bring out that information. They have typically been the ones that have brought humans closer to their souls with their bodies. Other mediums, other psychics, other spiritual people, other mystics have done it in other ways. But the physical trance mediums are the ones where the bodies are included. They provided the way for you to know and acknowledge soul. The physical trance mediums not only bring in soul but they bring in Earth soul. They have both dynamics going on."

Teacher

Chapter 12

DEATH BED
Makes one shudder at the choice of sealing embalmed bodies in thick fiberglass coffins, cast in a state of inertia, non-moving, non-giving back, in energy or information reserved for the Earth. A body disconnected from nature, the continuum and further becoming.

Chapter 12

WALKING INSIDE YOUR GREATER BODY EXERCISE
For the exercise to be effective, it's best performed outdoors, preferably in a quiet, natural setting far from buildings, traffic and technology.

Select a place you want to start. Face a direction or path you wish to walk. One that appears inviting to you. If a group - form a circle facing out.

To start, close your eyes and breathe easily.
Let your hands hang free and open at your sides.
Let go of mental chatter for the time being.
Simply be as you are.

When you're ready to begin, open your eyes and start walking freely— only you are no longer walking on the surface of the Earth. You are now walking inside of your greater body. A body that has trees and rivers inside it. A body that has mountains and oceans and planets and star fields. All around you is your inner world. The Greater You, the Greater Body.

Note how you feel as you walk about. Listen to the sounds, feel the energies above and below and around you. Give yourself permission to take all the time in the world.

Your only destination is to arrive here and now, with yourself connected to everything.

If your perception should stop or falter, let that be okay. Keep walking and allow this outside-is-inside point of view to return.

Ask yourself how this shift in perception changes the way you feel about the world. Are your senses heightened? Do you see other life forms more vividly in color, texture and aliveness? How does being in this state of mind make you feel about humanity? About your life and the work you do? How does it alter your personal sense of responsibility?

ACKNOWLEDGEMENTS

I am grateful to all my teachers and helpers, both physical and etheric, without whom I would not have grown in this awareness. I wish to extend loving thanks to my wife, Veronica, for her faithful support and tolerance during my energy explorations and experiments. I also wish to express my heartfelt thanks to Donna Fortune, for her insight, her truth, and her ocean of knowledge. And to the many friends who read the manuscript and provided helpful tips and guidance, especially when I veered too far afield for the uninitiated reader.